Hudson
Modern

David
Sokol

Hudson Modern

Residential Landscapes

THE MONACELLI PRESS

006
Introduction

010
Davis House

022
LM Guest House

038
Pound Ridge House

052
Stanfordville Guest House

064
Bedford Residence

076
Open House

088
Conversation with Andrew Zuckerman

The lure of the Hudson Valley is about space and freedom on a certain level. And there is this expansiveness in nature while having such proximity to enclosure and the city.

096
Artist's Studio

110
A House in the Woods

122
Red Rock House

136
Confluence House

148
Conversation with BarlisWedlick

What if we were to stop trying to make the woods pretty? The lesson is to let the landscape take care of itself. How has that lesson translated to designing homes?

156
Natori Residence

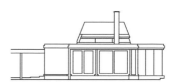

172
Old Field Farm

186
Dutchess County Art Barn

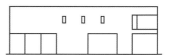

198
House 432

212
Ex of In House

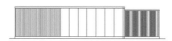

226
Conversation with Drew Lang

There's an inherent sense of community at Hudson Woods. Homeowners share this deep interest in the place, and from that commonality they want to connect with one another.

232
Hudson Guest House

244
The River House

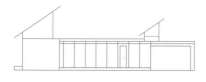

260
Acknowledgments & Credits

The Other Hudson River School

An area wide enough for the territory of a nation lies beneath you like an inlaid vein of silver. . . . The rich colors of the "garniture of the earth" stole out and the hundred towns within range of the eye glittered like studded gems over the scene. It looked like a distant Eden flooded with light.

So wrote a correspondent for *The Boston Recorder and Telegraph* about the Hudson River Valley in 1826, in a sunrise dispatch from the recently opened Catskill Mountain House. The reporter was most likely retracing the steps of white-hot artist Thomas Cole, who had stayed at the high-altitude hotel the prior year, and whose paintings based on that visit were catapulting the then-twenty-five-year-old to fame. At about the same time Bostonians were reading about the hotel's "transcendent" vista, multiple periodicals had printed rave reviews of Cole's depictions of Catskill and Cold Spring, New York. Was this wunderkind the real deal, or a youngster whose fit of imagination had earned momentary attention? *The Recorder* stood in Cole's shoes, deeming the scenery heavenly and its documentarian a genius.

The landscape straddling the Hudson River between Albany and the northern edge of New York City alternates between placidness and drama.

The rest seems fairly well inscribed in history. Although Cole admitted to a patron, "the most lovely and perfect parts of Nature may be brought together, and combined in a while that shall surpass in beauty and effect any picture painted from a single view," the Hudson Valley at least provided excellent source material for his work. The landscape straddling the Hudson River between between Albany and the northern edge of New York City alternates between placidness and drama and, by turning up the volume on that give-and-take, Cole secured his cultural standing quickly. And artists such as Albert Bierstadt and Frederic Edwin Church followed him to the region, painting its pastoral meadows and forested mountains also to idyllic and career-making effect. Together, these artists coalesced into the Hudson River School, and they prompted a larger, uniquely American dialogue about the sublime that informed the nation's industrialization, westward expansion, and artistic identity.

The Hudson River School is not suspended in amber; its history continues to unfold. Not far from one of the world's most dynamic and built-up cities persists a world of knife-like crests and gentle plains, rugged forests and tapestries of farmland. As Calvin Tsao, while discussing the Tsao & McKown–designed Natori Residence (page 156), explains, "Although we have seen a lot of suburban expansion, it is nothing compared to most places, where sprawl is contaminating." Few global metropolitan regions have preserved the distinction between the urban and the rural as have New York City and the Hudson Valley.

The valley's landscape transfixes much like it did almost two centuries ago, as well. To be sure, Cole's proto-Photoshop work would be cut out for him nowadays: the view from Pine Orchard, where Catskill Mountain House once hovered 1,600 feet above the Hudson River, is interrupted by far more development. But Tsao's comment remains emblematic and true. The Hudson Valley possesses an inherent beauty that moves people. Moreover, it moves people to document (perhaps with alterations) its enchanting combination of topography, habitat, and daylight in art.

The Hudson Valley's ongoing role as a cradle of art may very well be the launch pad for this book. Residential architecture is a creative act, and one could argue that a Hudson River School for architecture developed alongside the famous paintings.

Fine arts' longstanding enthusiasm for the Hudson Valley is predicated not on the region's nature alone, but on how manmade imprints like architecture and engineering throw nature into relief. The *Boston Recorder and Telegraph* staffer wrote of the hundred towns in his sight; Cole punctuated his canvases with agricultural and industrial imagery; the infatuation with the

The Hudson Valley's ongoing role as a cradle of art may very well be the launch pad for this book.

Hudson Valley in the nineteenth century relied fundamentally on geographic access, namely the opening of the Erie Canal. Simply put, the taming of wilderness factors significantly in the artistic representation of wilderness. The symbiosis between art and architecture in turn spawns more of both. We can imagine ourselves flocking to this landscape with enthusiasm, because the landscape had already been redesigned for our comfort.

The design itself was groundbreaking. While images of architecture helped convey the benign quality of the Hudson Valley landscape in fine art, the region's bricks-and-mortar architecture consistently had its boundaries tested in the name of engaging landscape. Take the Catskill Mountain House, which spawned marvels like a funicular for transporting guests, expediting their communion with nature. On the scale of the domicile, consider Alexander Jackson Downing. This son of Newburgh, New York, devoted a goodly part of his career to popularizing the front porch, so that residents of his cottages could more casually benefit from trees and fresh air—a progression toward modernism's tenet of bringing the outdoors in. Several decades later, a collective of young New Yorkers tapped Frank Lloyd Wright to plan a community that felt like an extension of the landscape, which today is the Usonian Historic District in Pleasantville, New York.

Ever since the Harvard Five settled in New Canaan, Connecticut, in the 1940s, corners of the greater New York area have become oases of cutting-edge, site-specific architecture. Modernism crystallized into a cosmopolitan suburb in New Canaan. Architects Harry Bates, Horace Gifford, and Andrew Geller adapted the movement's underlying principles to the why-not informality of Fire Island. Charles Gwathmey assayed modernism for the Hamptons shortly thereafter, launching a phenomenon that takes multiple forms to this day. At the opening of the twenty-first century, this enclave narrative will finally center on the Hudson Valley. The projects featured in *Hudson Modern* respond to the milieu in a way that is both coherent as a group and separate from other New York–area modernism hotspots. KieranTimberlake applied profound thought to produce a uniquely site-specific design in Pound Ridge, New York, for instance (page 038), and Michael Haverland eschewed his cosmopolitan design vocabulary to suit the poetry of agricultural land for artist Peter Nadin and his wife Anne Kennedy (page 172). These buildings represent energizing dialogues between the Cartesian and the organic, and they have reached critical mass, arguably after generations of gestation. They bring to fruition the other Hudson River School.

Without claiming any definitiveness, this book will help the Hudson Valley's homeowners, architects, and design observers determine exactly what distinguishes its present-day modernism from historic New Canaan modernism or ongoing Hamptons modernism, or even from the smaller bursts of modernism and proto-modernism that took place in the Hudson Valley previously. Responsiveness to landscape conditions is only one such criterion. The houses in *Hudson Modern* embody a nuanced awareness of regional architectural history. They also uniquely serve digital-era occupants: the new dwellings of the Hudson Valley offer escape from urban hustle, but also opportunities that range from artistic practice and ethical agricultural production to creative reflection; in contrast to the more hedonistic traits of a modernist incubator like Palm Springs, today's Hudson Valley architecture seeks to flatter both body and mind. Finally, the residences featured in the following chapters are modest in both degree and kind. They seek to preserve the transcendent landscape not merely by providing counterpoint to it, but by consistently opting for unimposing size and minimal spectacle.

Perhaps this last point is mere coincidence, but it may also be the most important. Aside from prompting a specific architectural response, digitization has helped unleash development energy in the Hudson Valley. Onlookers have now dubbed the region a new Hamptons or New York City's sixth borough, and headline-making growth often equates insensitive consumption—an aggressive erasure of what had charmed a place to begin with. In exemplifying respect for history, site specificity, and overall modesty, the houses of *Hudson Modern* attempt to define Eden for our generation. They may very well steer the region more closely toward it, too.

Davis House

When Sharon Davis's daughter turned twelve years old, the New York–based architect realized that time was running out to build her a treehouse at their summer home in Garrison, New York. The preteen knew as much, and asked her mother to create a design with more grown-up appeal: the hideaway had to appear impenetrable to bothersome youngsters, and include spaces for socializing, writing, and contemplating the landscape. Davis fulfilled her duties to the little client in 2013.

When Davis began designing a new house across the street at about the same time, analogous criteria held sway. To be constructed on the foundation of a shed adjacent to a clapboard barn, the house needed to screen occupants from passersby, maximize utility, and embrace nature.

"I set myself the challenge of only building on the shed's footprint, to avoid disturbing the surrounding landscape," Davis says, concluding that existing conditions dictated similar goals for the home as much as hereditary predisposition. Take privacy. Because the abandoned shed hugs the colonial-era Old Albany Post Road immediately to the west, transforming it into an all-glass beacon would have inserted car traffic into the domestic realm. Giving the new building a more inaccessible cloak would also better sympathize with historic postal-route structures and prevent interior electric light from piercing the night sky.

Davis responded to these measures first by layering a retaining wall on top of the old foundation, to raise the house's main rooms well above the rolling landscape. She fashioned a one-and-a-half-story volume atop that, finishing it with an angled roof to harmonize with the profile of the extant barn. A flat-roofed, one-story kitchen connects to the taller volume at a right angle, forming an L that outlines a patio.

—
Architect Sharon Davis surveys the landscape
from her rooftop deck.

Section and plan only half-describe the architect's effort. The elevations of the house that are visible from Old Albany Post Road are finished in salvaged Douglas fir and sport relatively little fenestration. Facades looking away from the road, meanwhile, are installed with fully retractable glass doors that profoundly meld outdoors and in. On the ground floor, the crook of the L slides away entirely, blurring the boundaries between the patio and kitchen and living area. Upstairs, a comparable door connects the floor-through master bedroom suite with the kitchen rooftop turned deck.

Davis's pairing of fir and glass captivates the newcomer, as he rounds a corner to see the house reveal itself like a cracked-open geode. The 900-square-foot interior produces its own set of delights. "I think of the circulation in this space as a spiral," Davis says, "You come in to the lower area from the front door and then the black steel staircase takes you up to the second floor, so you're always facing the view." Continually looking at Davis's patio and acreage makes the home feel much larger than its square footage. To reinforce the impression of seamless indoor-outdoor connection, landscape architect Nelson Byrd Woltz devised a site-built stone wall that draws the eye far to the east; in a similar vein, Davis suspended the master bedroom across the upper story so that daylight would cascade downstairs.

Davis's focus on the outdoors not only effects spaciousness, but also embodies the respect for place that originally motivated her to go small. Other evidence of that sensitivity is ecological. Interior millwork is made from reclaimed local oak, heating and cooling is geothermal, and soy foam insulates the building.

Ultimately, Davis reflects, these are self-indulgences with a political dimension, rather than vice versa. "Certainly, this was an experiment to see how much space I really needed to live, and how I could protest the McMansion phenomenon with a small environment whose beauty and luxuriousness provided me with fulfillment," she says of her treehouse 2.0. "Yet I'm also totally in love with the Hudson Valley. I found Garrison on my own and raised my kids here for more than twenty years, and the landscape and its history is a huge part of who I am at this point. There's no way it doesn't influence what I do. Even on an emotional level. Even without my being aware of it."

—
The master bedroom opens to a rooftop deck from which occupants can look outward, or consider the house interior.

—

"Certainly, this was an experiment to see how I could protest the McMansion phenomenon."

—
The master bedroom includes a glass-enclosed bath (opposite).
The ground-floor interior seamlessly combines living and kitchen zones (above).

—
Davis House neighbors an extant clapboard-covered barn.

LM
Guest
House

The task of designing a house means fulfilling a home-owner's needs, keeping within a budget, and making a scheme come to fruition. In privileged cases, a client will challenge her architect to create something that is also a cultural contribution. LM Guest House is one of those instances, and its design by Desai Chia Architecture squares the history of modern architecture with a building language authentic to the Hudson Valley. Specifically, it rethinks the Farnsworth House, the 1951 glass-enclosed residence by Ludwig Mies van der Rohe that occupies a place in the discipline's pantheon.

The Farnsworth House, located on the rural fringe of Chicago, comprises low-slung forms that appear to hover above a riverside landscape. It is as stunning a commentary on personal identity in an industrialized world as it is a visual composition. Yet icons are not without their flaws. Katherine Chia, who runs Desai Chia with Arjun Desai, says the facade technology that allowed mid-twentieth-century houses to effectively disappear into nature did not resist temperature swings or UV damage. She also notes that the Farnsworth House was designed for a single doctor as a weekend haven, limiting its adaptability to different patterns of living.

So, when young parents approached Desai Chia to realize a sustainable guesthouse on a 360-acre working farm in Dutchess County, citing the Farnsworth House among their inspirations, the New York–based studio conceived the project as that landmark's enlightened progeny. Desai Chia embraced state-of-the-art green technologies to blur indoors and out without discomfort, and it solved the Farnsworth House's occupancy problem by accommodating a family of four and two guests in a similar footprint.

At first glance, LM Guest House and the Farnsworth House have more commonalities than differences. Both are rectilinear, rest lightly on their lots, overlook bodies of water, and contain asymmetrically placed cores that contain kitchens and bathrooms. Scrutiny reveals Desai Chia pushing and pulling at the precedent in quiet, yet assertive, ways.

—
LM Guest House emits a lantern-like glow after dark.

Most important among these reconsiderations, a much-enlarged core packs more uses and people into 2,000 square feet than wide-open interiors could accomplish alone. Here the core contains two sleeping areas filled with bunkbeds, a pair of storage spaces, and a mechanical room alongside a crisp-lined bathroom. Desai and Chia collaborated with engineers at Arup to embed four steel columns within the core, as well; the roof cantilevers from the core, so that the prefabricated glass skin lacks the Farnsworth House's visible structure. The new facade comprises triple-pane glass units to withstand the sun's rays as well as extreme hot and cold; automated, digitally controlled interior shades provide privacy or an extra layer of solar protection to the glass.

The larger core gives the perimeter master bedroom, living room, and circulation spaces unfettered visual access to the farm, which was designed by Michael Van Valkenburgh Associates. Design details at the building edge amplify the sense of immersion in landscape. Individual glass units are extended above and below floor and ceiling, placing their frames out of sight. Manmade distractions like ductwork and light fixtures are hidden away in the raised floor and lowered ceiling (which also contain active sustainability technologies that include geothermal heating and photovoltaic infrastructure). That breezes may flow through operable windows in the facade adds tactility to one's perception that nature is permeating shelter.

By enclosing the core partly in slatted oak, Desai Chia extended the experience of nature to kids and guests. One can wake up to dappled sunlight, natural ventilation, and birdsong from a bunkbed. The porous surfaces work in tandem with the interior's bullseye-like organization to social effect, as well, by engendering occupants' sensitivity to others' presence and compelling people to convene.

LM Guest House's dual embrace of nature and community has resonated deeply with the homeowners, who have deferred erecting a salvaged barn on the property as their main residence. The design likely strikes a chord with any family that longs to interact with nature and one another. In fact, it may just inspire the next generation of glass houses.

—
The house is set within an agricultural
landscape encompassing 360 acres.

—
The master bedroom is immersed in the landscape,
yet maintains a sense of privacy.

—

Scrutiny reveals Desai Chia pushing and pulling at the precedent in quiet, yet assertive, ways.

A central core includes two sets of bunkbeds (above), and shares a partition
wall with the kitchen that overlooks the living room (opposite).

—
Two exterior views into LM Guest House's living room.

Interior partitions never intersect with the building perimeter.

Pound Ridge House

Analyzing precedent forms an early step in every designer's creative process. When faced with a house commission, architects return time and again to two forerunners: the Mies van der Rohe–designed Farnsworth House in Plano, Illinois, and the Glass House in New Canaan, Connecticut, that Philip Johnson completed for himself in 1949. Among other lessons, these midcentury landmarks assert that floor-to-ceiling glass allows a modern home to commune with nature authentically. Pound Ridge Residence, designed by KieranTimberlake for Mike and Olga Kagan, poses an alternative method in which a facade may be opaque, reflective, see-through, and glimmering all at once.

The Glass House has become so synonymous with the melding of architecture and landscape that, when the Kagans tapped KieranTimberlake to conceive what the Philadelphia-based firm's partner Jason Smith calls "a house *of* the woods, not just in the woods," it provided an instant mutual reference. Besides being located several miles from the client's 30-acre Westchester County site, Smith says "it was the manner in which the environment sees in to the Glass House, and the way the house sees out" that demanded considering the 1,800-square-foot building as this project's lodestar.

Field evidence suggested otherwise. Combing the 100-foot glacial escarpment in person, Smith and company namesake Stephen Kieran found a pair of "rooms" separated by a small ravine near the boulder-strewn ridgetop that, Kieran remembers telling the husband and wife, "is almost as if the site has been awaiting their home for 15,000 years."

Placing a two-story rectilinear volume in the lower room, and a single-story counterpart in the room above, promised to accommodate both 5,000 square feet of living space and a reverence for landscape. "The fit is that tight and that right, with the rock cliffs enveloping the dwelling in a rich, sculptural conversation between geological place and manmade space," Kieran notes. Whereas Johnson's singular pavilion surveys an idyll, these two buildings would become extensions of the craggy terrain connected by a glass bridge.

Deep engagement with site also led to reevaluating the Glass House's prevailing material. The single-paned New Canaan residence leaks like a sieve and, Smith says, "We came quite quickly to the fact that a standard vocabulary of residential modernism could not easily yield comfort and energy efficiency. We would have to build a house mostly with solid, and not much void."

—

Pound Ridge House comprises two volumes that
are connected by bridge.

Due to its siting, structure and skin are constructed using only materials that were movable by small gantry or hand. The difficult conditions dictated a straightforward assembly of structural insulated panels on insulated slabs on grade. They also yielded a visually energetic solution for a high-performing building envelope. Above each volume's stone-clad base is a tapestry of brushed and polished stainless steel mounted over aluminum honeycomb, as well as lead-coated copper panels and glass. "We wanted the facade strategy to be dynamic and playful, to reflect the geometry of the glacial site in a way that purely orthogonal construction logic could not," Smith says. Moreover, the design forces introspection about one's relationship to nature: reflective steel at the corners questions the boundary between built and natural environments, and the exterior materials capture changes of time and season.

Weathertight windows comprise only 13 percent of this outer surface, and rigorous calculation minimized wasted sheet metal.

Pound Ridge Residence translates this experience of site to the interiors. Entering the northernmost volume at grade, one notes how its stairway transitions from concrete to white oak to celebrate the act of ascent. The glass bridge's flood of light draws movement from north to south. Sparing windows frame an adjacent boulder or long-range view as tree trunks might. In all, "The home is very much the culmination of a carefully crafted journey up and across the glacial terrain," says Stephen Kieran, "the distinction between natural and artificial becomes mute." It makes the environmental immersiveness of the Glass House seem almost rudimentary in comparison.

—
The building nests into the creases of a glacial escarpment.

—

"It is almost as if the site has been awaiting their home for 15,000 years."

—
The living area (opposite) is reached via stair whose different
materials correspond with height (above).

The volumes open to the landscape in a curated manner, and their reflective
surfaces blur the boundary between built and natural environments.

—
Besides employing reflective surfaces, Pound Ridge House uses slim
dimensions and rustic materials to disappear into the landscape.

Stanfordville Guest House

The Hudson Valley has been a proving ground for modernism since the movement's inception. To be sure, upstate New York's claim on twentieth-century architecture is not as celebrated as those of New Canaan, Connecticut, or the resort communities of Fire Island. Yet the Marcel Breuer–designed McComb House or Russel Wright's Manitoga, respectively located in Poughkeepsie and Garrison, compare with the Glass House and the collective work of Horace Gifford and Andrew Geller as experiments in site-specific form. Manhattan-based Alan Orenbuch and Bryan O'Rourke are custodians of the Hudson Valley's modernist legacy.

The architect and interior designer purchased Plastic Tent House in Stanfordville, New York, in 2009 after a decade-long search for an upgrade from their Clinton Corners bungalow. Also known as Johansen House #2, the residence is the work of Harvard Five architect John Johansen, and a unique illustration of the Hudson Valley's historic progressive architecture.

Designed in 1974 and entirely rebuilt after a fire the following year, the Plastic Tent House served as a rural retreat for Johansen and his wife Ati Gropius Johansen. The building resembles a table-cut diamond in translucent plastic, and sports various projections like a patio and bridge. Inside, three suspended floors linked by a spiral staircase form interlocking double-height spaces in which the master bedroom and structural supports are fully exposed. Locally sourced stone on the ground floor inserts landscape into the playground-like interior. "It isn't completely worked out—the corners have no real function and you hit your head on some ceilings—yet John is a genius for bringing together influences ranging from Le Corbusier to Frank Lloyd Wright to Archigram," Orenbuch says.

While enthralled by the Plastic Tent House's voluminous interior and exciting section, framing of Catskills views, and park-like setting, as new homeowners Orenbuch and O'Rourke were consistently reminded of its drawbacks. The Plastic Tent House's single Jack and Jill bathroom made hosting duties cramped and un-private, and its signature material diffuses rather than blocks daylight, problematic in the case of the sleeping loft. After suffering a visit from a clamorous friend, it was decided to convert Johansen's nearby shed into a guest house.

The former shed's east-facing entry is accessible via
modest footbridge.

Johansen had designed that building with shoebox proportions so as not to compete with the main residence, then expanded it westward twice to accommodate his jewelry workshop and Gropius Johansen's papermaking studio. O'Rourke and Orenbuch stored antiques and salvaged appliances there, but saw potential beyond the brown- and purple-painted planks and haphazard additions. "Just as the Plastic Tent House's middle level connects to the hillside via a bridge, an entry bridge takes you from a parking area to the shed's east elevation, as the site slips underneath the building," Orenbuch says, "That gives it the semblance of a gatehouse." And although the west elevation was finished in two cheap, off-the-shelf windows, they did offer a stunning view of layered hills giving way to the Catskill Mountains. Johansen clearly had devoted considerable thought, if not the dollars, to making the shed livable.

To clarify a new, domestic use, Orenbuch first removed the two carbuncles from the west elevation. Subtraction revealed a quintessential modernist composition. Cantilevering from a cinderblock plinth that wedges into the hillside, the one-story rectilinear volume appears to emerge from the slope like an oversize stereoscope.

Orenbuch then determined that the stripped-away west elevation should be fully glazed, to open to the view and maximize daylight penetration within the original 385 square feet. He backed the bathroom against the east elevation to keep interior partitions from interfering with that window wall, and arranged a bedroom and the living room to bookend a kitchenette along the uninterrupted glass. The size and configuration of the windows were influenced by various midcentury precedents in the Hudson Valley and elsewhere.

There was a notion of making the guest house more like the Plastic Tent House, by means of balconies and other elements. The extra work would have complicated approval processes and increased costs, however. Today Orenbuch appreciates the romantic benefits of taking the simpler path, which was fully realized in 2014. The guest house offers panoramic views distinct from the Plastic Tent House's atmospheric filtering of the sun. That the reused building lacks outdoor space even encourages socializing in some cases, as it compels nature-loving visitors to seek their hosts on the main residence's patio.

By relieving pressure on the Plastic Tent House, the updated guest house also makes historical stewardship easier. Orenbuch and O'Rourke have changed the main residence—removing the original cantilevered platform in the guest room, turning the hot tub into a planter—in ways that better cater to their lives, but which also can be easily reinstated by future owners. Compared to the recent demolition of several Johansen buildings, these reversible revisions are a boon to the latest movement in modernist architecture—preserving it.

The fully glazed west elevation helps the Stanfordville Guest House interior feel much larger than its 385 square feet.

—

The one-story rectilinear volume appears to emerge from the slope like an oversize stereoscope.

A bedroom (opposite) and living room (above) trace the west-
facing wall of glass; a kitchenette sits between them.

Stanfordville Guest House's stereoscope-like west
elevation, seen from outside.

Bedford Residence

While modernism has long been at home in the Hudson Valley, it has washed over the region in identifiable waves. During a rush of architectural activity in the early 2000s, for example, architects employed overtly progressive building shapes to enhance the relationship between occupant and site. For the 2012 renovation of a weekend home in Bedford, New York, one architect who participated in the early-2000s groundswell, Joel Sanders, expanded the terms of successful design to include rootedness in habitat and history, as well as exceptional form.

Sanders joined the Hudson Valley's first wave of 21st-century modernists when he was asked to conceive a new house in Hudson, New York, not far from Olana. The deftness with which the landmark home and studio of Frederic Edwin Church frames vistas of the Hudson Valley resonated with Sanders's self-professed interest "in looking at buildings as platforms." In response, the New York architect organized his project, called House on Mt. Merino, around an interior courtyard nestled into the mountainside, to master views to the south and west.

The manner in which House on Mt. Merino leveraged its sloping site sparked a new curiosity within Sanders: Why do architects and landscape architects rarely collaborate as equals? He shared this query with his friend the late Diana Balmori, the prominent landscape and urban designer, and the pair initiated a class at Yale as well as a book project called *Groundwork* (which this publisher released in 2011) to propose a more integrated design process. Simultaneously, Bedford Residence's owners contacted Sanders for assistance.

Architect William H. Switzer had originally completed Bedford Residence as a second home for the then-head of Mutual Life Insurance of New York and his wife in 1959, and the current client had become deeply aware of the mid-century design's charms and flaws over years of weekend use. While the 3,000-square-foot main residence and 550-square-foot pool house complemented the wooded 4-acre site, small windows, deep eaves, and an old-fashioned kitchen kept sunshine and scenery at arm's length.

If the husband and wife initially thought Sanders would make surgical improvements like removing the kitchen, an engineer discovered structural and material deficiencies that demanded a more ambitious scope of work. Reconstruction of the primary wood-framed structure and razing and rebuilding the pool and pool house were all required. When Sanders proposed using the opportunity to weave inside and out in collaboration with Balmori, "The client really became patrons of an interface design approach," the architect recalls. "It became very important to them to execute this concept, and they're very proud of it."

—

Bedford Residence is a reinvention of a home originally
completed in 1959 by architect William H. Switzer.

The resulting renovation pays respect to Switzer's vision. The footprint remains a rotated L whose stem follows an east–west axis, and its massing parallels the topography just as before. The project expresses further historical continuity in its use of cedar and walnut cladding and stacked bluestone. On the other hand, Sanders removed interior partitions to bring in daylight and views. He also oriented the bi-level interior's lower and upper levels in opposite directions, to better differentiate them in the absence of walls.

While expanses of glass and steel in both of these spaces foster engagement with site, Sanders notes, "The main idea of this project was to come up with a palette of organic and inorganic materials that sweep you along that indoor-outdoor journey." Within a border of wood planks, the architect poured a "carpet" of concrete under the dining and living areas to demarcate their uses. The flooring works in tandem with a suspended sheetrock ceiling to direct views to the rear. It literally leads outdoors, as well, extending past the building envelope to form a dining patio and pavers that stretch to the pool. At one end of this sequence, the concrete folds upward to serve as a kitchen island, and at the other terminus the material encloses a new pool house that features a retractable glass wall.

Less refined ingredients complete the melding of natural and human worlds. Bluestone, gravel, and garden meet the concrete pavers in a frayed edge, and Balmori arranged the vegetation in concentric zones that give yield to the forest. In addition, Sanders surrounded the pool area in a fieldstone retaining wall that tapers into the earth, providing opportunities for sitting and lounging along the way.

Sanders could have simply relied on floor-to-ceiling windows to right Switzer's wrongs. He also could have crafted spaces as platforms for viewing the forest, a Mt. Merino Redux. Yet by partnering with Balmori on Bedford Residence, the architect engendered more intimacy between occupant and landscape. Bedford Residence's intractable sense of place is a testament to personal inquisitiveness and professional collaboration, and a defining characteristic of the current wave of Hudson Valley modernism.

—

Expansive glazing of the rear connects the house interior to
the pool area and to the landscape more generally.

—

"The main idea of this project was to come up with a palette of organic and inorganic materials that sweep you along that indoor-outdoor journey."

—
The living area employs a "carpet" of concrete to produce
continuity between interior vignettes and the outdoors.

073

—
The concrete carpet terminates in a new pool house, whose form and
materials depart from the mid-century vocabulary of the main residence.

Open House

Architects David Leven and Stella Betts are attracted to camping for its casual, deposit-yourself-where-you-wish quality; as Betts puts it, "You can engage the landscape in lots of different ways." Yet even campsites follow some general planning guidelines. Not unlike programming a house or zoning a city, where you pitch your tent is distinct from your cooking and eating sites. Over three years, the founders of New York–based LevenBetts spent weekends camping on a clearing of a 10-acre property just outside of Hudson, New York, and played with the loose prescriptions of campsite design. They jiggered with a tent platform, fire pit, trailer, and other stations until each related perfectly to its patch of meadow in the woods, and stood the just-right distance from water uses.

"We were fascinated by these separate islands of program—this idea of domesticated space within the landscape," Betts says of that period. The house that she and Leven more recently completed on the site translates the island concept to a single enclosure.

The partners in work and life started design of the 1,300-square-foot house, called Open House, just as they were brainstorming a new kind of building module for an exhibition curated by Andrew Zuckerman (page 088). The proposed module's footprint was shaped like a right trapezoid with a sixty-degree angle, and appears fully as a quarter-cube open on two ends. The result can flip or rotate into multiple configurations. "That then drove the idea of our house," Leven explains. "We thought of each volume as a room that captures one piece of the overall program."

Leven and Betts translated campsite uses into residential functions, then assigned one function per module. The campsite's poured-concrete fire pit became the module containing a kitchen, for example, and its stone patio the dining-room module. The modules were modified for construction efficiency as well as comfort—not so big that steel was required, and not claustrophobically small, either—and laid in an alternating pattern along a north–south axis. There are five ground-floor modules in total, and they interlock to form a rectangular footprint with a chamfer at one end. That series is topped by triangular bedroom and bathroom spaces bisected by a stair; the surrounding rooftop is planted with succulents.

—
Architects David Leven and Stella Betts designed Open
House for themselves just outside Hudson, New York.

Each volume also was conceived to produce a different relationship with the landscape. The kitchen reverse-tapers into the dawn light while the dining room reaches toward sunsets in a similar fashion, and the bathroom receives more diffuse north–south illumination. Leven and Betts preserved the outdoor shower, picnic table, and other favorite spots from the former campsite, to add dimension and energy to the scenes.

Because the modules' squeezing and decompressing gestures required compartmentalizing the interior, the exterior wall of each room is finished in floor-to-ceiling glass as well as a door "to encourage a strong connection to the outdoors and its extant domestic spaces," Betts says, "you can move in and out of the house without necessarily going through other interiors; every room becomes a porch." Leven adds, "You live on the entirety of the acreage, and the house is an

incident within that experience." The interior is clad almost completely in plywood while white stucco finishes the facades, to minimize distractions from the natural world.

Even in this permanent version of roughing it, there remains a casual quality. "You will weave between site and house in the summer, while winters will be devoted to weaving more tightly through the layout and contemplating the various views to which the windows are calibrated," Betts envisions. She and Leven have assured they can continue fine-tuning their living arrangements, as well. The modules are so loosely defined by their functions that the architects could decide to flip rooms around with minimal effort. As long as each room feels like the humble camping stations with which they first occupied this bit of paradise, they will know they are on the right path.

—
Although the house partly replaces a campsite, its porosity
to the outdoors honors the spirit of camping.

—

"We were fascinated by these separate islands of program— this idea of domesticated space within the landscape."

—
In plan, Open House comprises a series of wedge shapes, which the
staircase and other vertical elements make legible in section.

—
The house's apertures are like portals to extant campsite
spots, and to the wider landscape.

In 2005, Andrew Zuckerman and Nicole Bergen moved into a weekend residence designed by David Leven and Stella Betts (the architects and owners of Open House, page 076) for the crest of a wooded ridge on the west side of the Hudson River. The principals of LevenBetts refer to the 2,400-square-foot building as "an incident along the path" whose cantilevers, unstained cedar cladding, and lack of formal entry encourages occupants to move between house and 11-acre property with ease.

In the years since that house's completion, Zuckerman and Bergen have expanded their family as well as their presence in the art world. The couple returned to Leven and Betts to expand the original residence and conceive an adjacent guest house with studio space, in turn. The more recent project includes a cedar-clad cube that attaches to the main house via glass skybridge. The guest house is informed by Japanese principles: while the new freestanding building also appears cube-like, its cardboard-formed concrete in fact contains six elevations designed around bathing and fire tending. Overall, LevenBetts's expansion creates a new option for experiencing the site. It draws people beneath the skybridge and toward the guest house and a communal lawn—whereas the original building, by itself, invited more circuitous exploration of the landscape.

Here, Zuckerman eloquently provides the client's perspective on *Hudson Modern*. He expounds on his and Bergen's attraction to the Hudson Valley, and how contemporary architecture has informed their understanding of place and home.

Andrew Zuckerman

090

Artist
Andrew Zuckerman

Was your decision to settle in the Hudson Valley informed by other weekend enclaves—that a place like the Hamptons was too costly and too dense?

Did some more indescribable quality prompt you to consider settling in the Hudson Valley, as well?

If nature and landscape have an enormous impact on you, then could a campsite have accomplished the experience you're describing?

How did this collaboration start?

AZ   We bought the house because David and Stella showed it to us. And while we couldn't afford a studio apartment in Manhattan, we were able to have eleven acres and the first house LevenBetts ever completed.

AZ   The lure of the Hudson Valley is about space and freedom on a certain level. And there is this expansiveness in nature, while having such proximity to enclosure and the city. My wife and I felt the need to return to a certain connection with nature that we had lost living in the city. There was a certain psychological volume that we were missing. I find that, when we're in that retreat, our ideas are different, our relationship to each other is different, our ability to listen is different, the pace is different.

AZ   Niki and I are both fascinated by design and architecture, and we both craved living inside something that hadn't existed before. This question really comes down to a very long exchange and dialogue with David and Stella, which has included the studio I work in, exhibitions, and the buildings on the upstate property.

AZ   I worked for David's brother when I was in art school and he owned a coffee shop on Irving Place; David and Stella had done the interior. So, we met back then, when I was a kid, and we met again when our studios were in the same building. We just immediately connected. There's so much shared interest. David and Stella have so much knowledge that I don't have, and vice versa, that we have a true relationship based on sharing information and ideas. Even though our practices, aesthetics, and ambitions are entirely different. For the recently completed guest house, I was interested in pushing them into a space that they hadn't necessarily occupied. So, there were a lot of ideas about Japan, programmatically—how one uses the house and how one relates to the environment around it. Also I was interested in building toward how we saw ourselves living years into the future, how we wanted to welcome people, and how we wanted them to experience a stay with us.

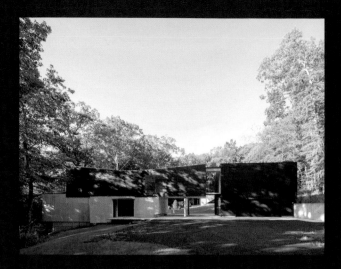

—
Zuckerman and
Nicole Bergen
recently tapped
LevenBetts to
expand a weekend
house the studio
had completed
in 2005.

Your programming needs were based on some practical realities, in that case.

By which you mean engaging the environment?

Would you say more about sensory experience?

How does the expansion of the main house contribute to this milieu?

AZ   We had a child and then another two children and the main house was just getting smaller and smaller, and we couldn't have guests yet we loved hosting lots of people. We were the first of all of our friends to have something outside of the city, and it became a place where we all got to see each other. I was very creative there, I made a film there. It became impossible to ignore needing two more bedrooms and a guest house. And it gave us a chance to play with ideas.

AZ   Everything about the guest house is about connection with place. The slab is six levels of elevation as it steps down the hill, and all the cabinetry was made from the white oak that was felled on site. We had the luxury of time, it being a guest house. We did it quite slowly and carefully. We did a lot of things that were certainly not practical decisions, but that ultimately serve the sensory experience of being there.

AZ   The house's relationship to the outdoors is a kind of constant activation. Because you have six levels of elevation, there's opportunity for discovery and shifts in perspective. The guest house is a theater for light and sounds are changing and you yourself are changing, from insulated to expansive feelings. The apertures in the house all frame specific elements, too. For example, by the soaking tub, a 10-by-10-foot glass door pockets into the house. Now imagine there's snow on the ground: you're almost outside but you're immersed in hot water. The guest house is this series of almost binary juxtapositions that wake you up. Ultimately, the project is about elements of beauty in the raw forest that are out of time, while the building is so clearly right now and so modern and technologically advanced. There's activation through contrast.

AZ   The skybridge came out of this idea that I didn't want to renovate the main house. I didn't want to erase the memory of it, of the choices that were made for it. I need to preserve that space and time, as a matter of personal history. In many ways, for Nikki and me this property is a kind of roadmap of our family life.

LevenBetts
simultaneously
realized a
poured-concrete
guesthouse on
the property.

Your thoughtfulness about the project's practical and spiritual goals is impressive. You set a high bar about what it means to be a good client.

And the work has paid off upstate.

Landscape architecture figures largely here, too.

What are the benefits of working with David and Stella repeatedly, versus engaging multiple architects for different commissions?

AZ   I wanted to be the most effective client I could be. And I remembered
      thinking, What did that mean? What is the responsibility of the client? I'm
      generally on the other side of it, I'm generally commissioned to do things,
      and I thought that it required a lot of work to be a great client. You couldn't
      just demand things or hope the architects read your mind or ask the right
      question. You have to present them with certain triggers for them to run
      with. It was about drawing out their highest ideas.

AZ   It's one of the few places I feel completely safe, where I have permission
      to completely turn off. Whereas in the city you're still driven by
      productivity and culture. I'm interested in finding a certain quiet. We
      are living in a time when it is hard for many people, including myself, to
      just figure out how you actually feel about something. I'm interested in
      stripping away self-criticism and the anxiety of influence, and figuring
      out what my authentic response to something is.

AZ   I don't think every building is architecture, I think architecture has to be
      somehow transformative in framing your experience with a surrounding
      area. David and Stella have certainly directed an experience of that land
      that makes you feel a certain way.

      The project would have been so different had Marc Keane not been
      part of it. I collect 17th-century *ikebana* scrolls, and what *ikebana*
      does is create a holistic representation of the universe with disparate
      elements—the representation of the world becomes scalable. There is
      a representation of *ikebana* in Marc's work that insinuates something
      larger than itself. I feel a connection to and understanding of something
      bigger, which changes the way I think, feel, and react.

AZ   They love my family and we love them; they know my children and
      understand how we are. We laugh a lot, we have fun together, we're
      friends. And they know that when they're doing these projects with us,
      they are defining a platform for our family to grow and live and be. Because
      our ongoing conversation is so personal, because they deeply understand
      our values and worldview, they're the only ones who could have worked on
      this home.

Artist's Studio

"A contrast of two vocabularies permits each to be stated most elegantly," says acclaimed artist Arlene Shechet. "To have a geometric shape next to a bulbous, bulging form is to make one aware of both." Just as Shechet's poignant, genre-defying ceramics incorporate contrasting shapes, so does her studio in Woodstock, New York.

The 1,750-square-foot extension to the James Meyers–designed house that Shechet shares with Mark Epstein was produced by architect Deborah Gans. "I love to work with artists, because they want their art to unfold in ways that are both spatial and haptic, without having the space compete with the art," the founder of Brooklyn-based Gans Studio says of designing homes and studios for artists. Elaborating on that thought, Shechet notes, "I have very strong ideas and aesthetics, and Deborah is someone who is going to work with me rather than for me."

During Shechet and Epstein's search for a Hudson Valley residence, they presumed that they would discover a nineteenth-century gem, next to which they would erect a barn-like structure as a studio.

Yet when the pair purchased the low-slung house that Meyers completed in 1964, the idea of a historically inspired addition suddenly seemed out of place. Gans, who had designed several workspaces for Shechet previously, was tapped to design a more appropriate, contemporary wing.

The relationship between the Meyers house and the defunct bluestone quarry on which it is sited informed the studio's conceptualization. The original, heavy timber–framed building perches atop a steep rise in the landscape, distancing occupants from a forest clearing with swimming pool to the north. Gans positioned the studio at the base of the outcropping, in turn, coordinating its width and length to the dimensions of the main house.

ARTIST'S STUDIO

The studio's ground floor is accessible by a long ramp
used for moving art materials.

The decision required excavating and reinforcing the hillside with a stone-finished retaining wall, and lifting the studio on concrete *pilotis* to prevent water damage from runoff. Though a slightly costlier approach, Shechet comments, "All of the property surrounding the main house was very beautiful. The exception was the view from the house to the space directly abutting it, which was a swampy pit. It was the only sensible place to dig into." Custom fiber-cement panels that clad the studio structure resemble the spacing between nearby trees, enhancing the new wing's verticality and making it appear as if it were reaching for the main house. Asymmetric fenestration evokes the dramatic topography.

Tucking the rectilinear volume next to the slope yields functional benefits to rival the aesthetic. The second floor of the main house connects exclusively to the studio's rooftop, where Shechet tends a sedum garden and uses a small glass-enclosed volume as a spray booth. She, Epstein, and their two grown children also convene at the roof's seating vignette to enjoy bird's-eye views of the forest clearing, as well as an introspective view back to Meyers's imprint. "Arlene wanted this project to be an asset for her family, and treating it as a green roof with a building underneath it gives back to the experience of the main house," Gans says.

Shechet devotes four days each week to practicing in Woodstock. She moves between life and work via a steel-framed footbridge that connects the ground floor of the house to the studio's mezzanine. Upon arriving in the studio, "You move down the stairs and diagonally across the studio toward the long, catty-cornered window," says Gans, adding that that "very layered promenade provides different orientations and scales for working." At the ramped lower-level entrance, the artist rolls raw materials and finished pieces in and out of the building.

The building actively supports Shechet's creative efforts further, thanks to mirrors mounted to clerestory windows that more evenly distribute incoming daylighting. The interior's reliance on natural ventilation for summertime cooling also nods to the barn Shechet had once envisioned. It is even tempting to say the studio embodies its owner's artistic point of view; the juxtaposition of crisp manmade form and craggy hillside seems sympathetic to Shechet's ceramic geometries. By making sure this project does not compete with the art, Gans invites the beholder's interpretation.

—
The composition of windows corresponds with
local topography.

—

The relationship between the Meyers house and the defunct bluestone quarry informed the studio's conceptualization.

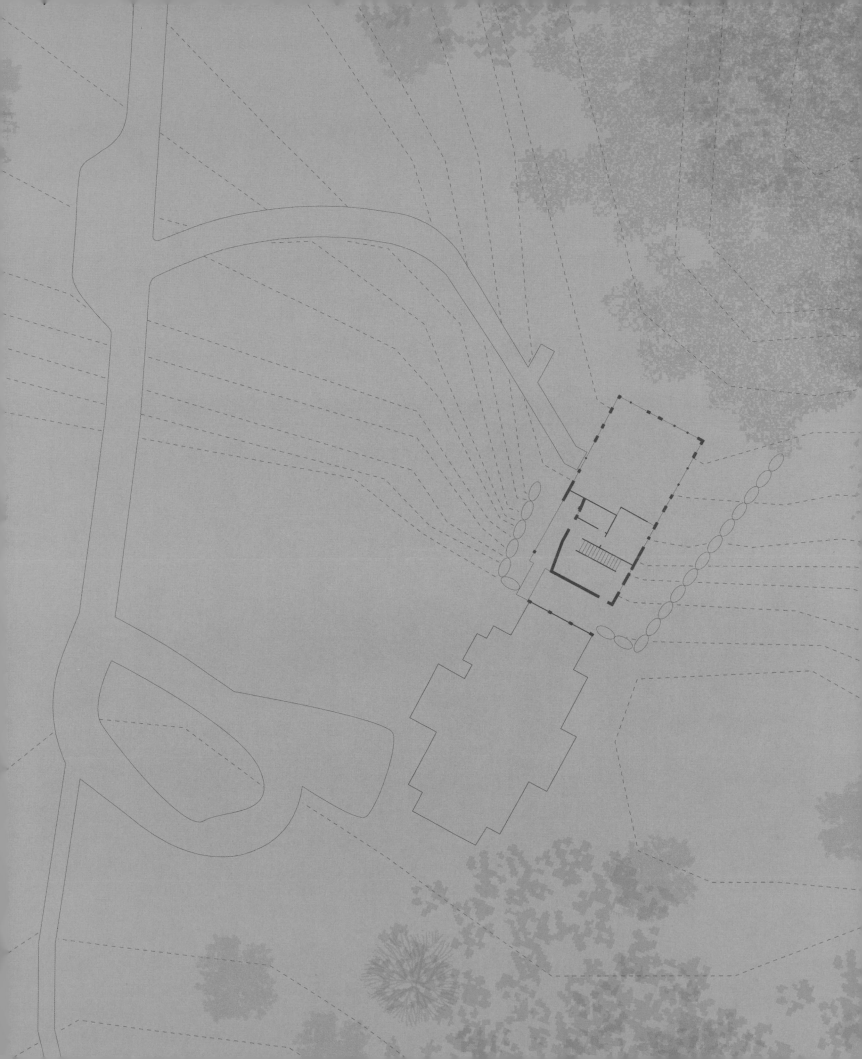

Fenestration offers selective views of nature and sky (left), which draw
occupants down from the mezzanine and into the studio (right).

The existing main residence connects to the studio via footbridges that
alight at the mezzanine (opposite) and roof (above).

Artist's Studio occupies a corner of a former quarry,
below the main residence.

A House in the Woods

However unintentional, design history is often a narrative of heroism, portraying architects as knowing all and acting alone. The story of this 4,800-square-foot weekend home in Ulster County, New York, by William Reue captures the more collaborative reality of design projects. The residence was a creative enterprise between the New York–based architect and the homeowner.

The client mulled this project for twenty-five years before formally commissioning a design from Reue in 2008, and by then she had made several key design decisions, such as purchasing wooded acreage at the base of the Shawangunk Mountains and devising a rough plan in which three distinct volumes are united by a curved Cor-Ten steel wall. She had also researched sustainability strategies, anointed the unbuilt project A House in the Woods, and interviewed multiple other architects for the job.

"I think we were chosen for our willingness to listen and work together," Reue recalls, explaining that the client had switched careers from corporate law to sustainable land use, and wanted to capture her environmentalism and overall character in three dimensions. Of form following self-expression, Reue says, "The conceit is unique to modern architecture—she was basically reprogramming her existence through this house. It was up to us to determine how to do it gracefully."

To reconcile long-gestating ideas to executable reality, the architect consolidated the three-part plan into one rectilinear volume that follows a southwest–northeast axis. The move best accommodated valley views to the south and east, and reduced the amount of building envelope exposed to the elements to improve energy efficiency. The house is assembled from fourteen-inch-thick structural insulated panels and clad primarily in local bluestone.

While the project's plan submitted to Reue's logic, the weathering steel wall was not to be debated. Measuring 125 feet long and twenty-four feet tall at its highest point, it originates south of the inhabitable spaces, appearing as an extension of the row of Norway spruces lining the driveway. It then veers into the rectilinear volume, and reemerges to point almost due north. Forecourts occupy the splays between curving steel and linear bluestone.

—
One long side of A House in the Woods includes a monumental Cor-Ten wall
whose patterning evokes colors and textures in nature.

In addition to creating a pair of impressive out-door rooms, the Cor-Ten wall orchestrates the first impressions of A House in the Woods. The wall's monumental dimensions shield the long west ele-vation of the house, conveying refuge for those within. It also stokes the anticipation of guests as they trace the driveway to the formal entry inside the northern forecourt—perhaps noticing all the while how the forest floor is repeated in the irreg-ularly patterned, earth-hued steel.

The wall's counterpart is a 65-by-13-foot expanse of quadruple-paned glass that floods the east-facing great room and adjoining master bedroom in day-light. On the residence's exterior, Reue placed this glass wall within a projecting cementboard-clad volume. Where the cantilever intersects with the house, Reue peeled away strips of bluestone and put long windows in their place. "It was important for the parts to read as discrete sculptural elements, so that the house didn't become a massive subur-ban block that ignores the scale of the landscape," he explains of articulating the east elevation.

For the occupant, these various moves make the great room and master bedroom "seem as if you're sitting inside binoculars," as Reue phrases it. "Hovering above the ground, watching the squir-rels and chipmunks, is like being in the middle of a zoo." Nature suffuses through the open-plan inte-rior, and causes the protective steel wall to largely fade from memory. In fact, the curving form only appears in the interior subtly, to suggest where public space gives way to bedrooms.

A House in the Woods rewards the winding, mys-terious journey to its entrance with a haven for watching the passing of wildlife and seasons. And if it removes the visitor ever so slightly from the landscape like an observation deck, it completely enmeshes her in the homeowner's emotional life. Reue says of the client, "What I love about this house is that once the front door is opened and you are welcomed in, all of the boundaries melt away. Once you understand this house, you under-stand her."

—
Tucked between the steel wall and the inhabitable volume is a pair
of forecourts, where a visitor will also find the formal entry.

—

"It was important for the parts to read as discrete sculptural elements, so that the house didn't become a massive suburban block that ignores the scale of the landscape."

—
Bucking first impressions, the residence's interior is
emphatically open to landscape.

—

The rear elevation of A House in the Woods appears to
hover slightly above the forested hillside.

Red
Rock
House

Anmahian Winton Architects is "hard to pin down," as cofounder Nick Winton puts it. "Some people would struggle to classify us, which is how we like it. Our work is deeply informed by site and program, as well as local building culture and available technologies." The Cambridge, Massachusetts–based studio's work ranges from an office tower in Ankara, Turkey, whose shading devices evoke *mashrabiyas*, to a private observatory in New Hampshire in which crystalline facets replace the traditional dome.

That Anmahian Winton avoids signatures has allowed the studio to think of its Hudson Valley commissions as an ongoing investigation of the region's character, and of how to express it architecturally. "The more time we spend there, the more we get influenced by the context, and the more the next house is finely tuned to the area," Winton observes. He adds that two conditions have prevailed throughout this effort. "First of all, there's a strong culture of modern, progressive thinking. Second, a design must reconcile culture with the untamed landscape."

Tapped by a husband and wife to design a prototype kit-of-parts house in the hamlet of Red Rock, New York, Winton encountered a rugged site epitomizing his second condition. "Wooded, rocky, and steep, it wasn't very hospitable at all," the architect remembers of the sixteen acres that the client had purchased in 2007. Upon completion six years later, Red Rock House manifested both culture and landscape.

Collaborating with the landscape architecture firm Reed Hilderbrand, Anmahian Winton ironed out some of the Red Rock property's resistance to construction, by erecting a north–south masonry wall that holds back the dramatic slope to the east for 200 feet. It then situated a 4,700-square-foot main residence along an east–west axis on the resulting meadow, and hemmed a two-bedroom guest house and sleek pergola to the retaining wall. The grassy plateau extends south to the road, and descends to the west in a long pleat of earth.

—
Red Rock House's underside illustrates how the design simultaneously
blends into the landscape and declares itself manmade.

Organizing Red Rock House as a compound engenders a feeling of safe arrival, as it recalls the image of a fairy-tale glade. The configuration is also highly practical, separating guests from the homeowners, who use the main residence intensively—her millinery studio occupies almost all of a partly submerged cellar, and the upper floor is divided between the sole bedroom and space for his expansive music collection. Friends and family have a freestanding domain to call their own, and the twain may meet in the shade of the pergola or within the main residence's art-filled entry level, which largely lacks partitions to encourage casual interaction.

How Anmahian Winton translated the main residence's plan into a composition of volumes again addresses the dialectic of culture and nature. "The house is slightly embedded in the landscape; it doesn't grossly clear a huge area," Winton says of trying to make a respectful intervention. To further prevent the building from appearing intrusive, the design team divided it into two smaller-scale volumes that slide past one another and beyond the plinth-like cellar. A bluestone pathway connecting the compound to the main residence forms a third gesture, and it cantilevers even farther to the west to become a balcony in the treetops. Muscular structure is plainly visible on the balcony's underside, intimating that even the most site-sensitive gestures are still unavoidably human.

The building envelope grapples with binaries, as well. Expanses of opacity and transparency suggest groundedness and flight. Pairing of machined aluminum and knotty cedar aligns modernity with rusticity.

Early in Red Rock House's gestation, the client banished the concept of prototyping a house-cum-product for sale. As the couple's love of the site and the budding design usurped a vision of real-estate entrepreneurship, so, Winton says, "The project went from being formal and speculative to highly personal and programmatic." Even in this highly intimate iteration, the house remains a model for Anmahian Winton, whose subsequent work in the Hudson Valley has allowed it to continue investigating the give-and-take of regional expression.

—
The cellar-level millinery studio opens to a lower lawn.

—

"The house is slightly embedded in the landscape; it doesn't grossly clear a huge area."

Views of the millinery studio (left) and first-floor
living area (right).

—

The main house is accompanied by a guest house and
pergola (opposite), which trace a retaining wall (above).

—
Red Rock House's full, complex geometry is withheld from
the visitor coming up the driveway for the first time.

Confluence House

As managing editor of the website Design Observer, Jade-Snow Carroll could have dialed up almost anyone to produce an avant-garde residence in the Hudson Valley. But myriad contacts were no match for serendipity—which, while snowshoeing through the woods of Columbia County, brought her to a bold, albeit familiar, building that seemed perfectly suited to emulation. The digerata slipped a note under the door to request information about the designer.

Carroll learned that the steel-and-wood creation was the work of Manhattan-based design firm Incorporated. When she and husband Ian Rasch tapped Incorporated for their own collaboration, they in fact signed up to participate in an ongoing experiment. Incorporated cofounder Adam Rolston had been trying to create an archetypal modern dwelling for the Hudson Valley, of which Carroll's discovery was just one result.

Rolston's search for a regionalist ideal began in the early 2000s. While biking and jogging on weekend visits with friends, the architect remembers, "I kept seeing a single-slope barn type that allowed dairy farmers to load hay into the barn underneath the roof's highest point." When he decided to stake his own claim in upstate New York, he began designing a 1,350-square-foot structure for a thicket in Hillsdale that expressed kinship with those barns.

The product of his work, called Sixteen Doors House, naturally features a single-slope roof. This steep pitch crowns eight facing pairs of sliding doors, and remaining vertical surfaces are clad in pine planks stained black. Rolston notes how his composition channeled local vernacular as well as the Craig Ellwood–influenced spaces remembered from his California childhood. It also acknowledged budgetary reality, namely by working within the dimensional constraints of wood construction to avoid expensive steel.

Incorporated has designed and constructed three additional mono-pitch homes since Sixteen Doors' completion in 2005, and of them, Carroll and Rasch's home, called Confluence House, was completed in Harlemville in 2013. Confluence House illustrates how the studio adapted Rolston's first, personal retreat to various clients and conditions.

—
The south face of Confluence House caps the gradual
rise of a meadow.

"We're in a moment when materiality is grounding," Rolston says of differentiating projects from one another. He notes that Confluence House's shiplap cypress is bleached and treated in a weathering stain to reflect the gray bark of nearby birch, maple, and oak trees. A standing-seam composite of zinc, magnesium, and aluminum covers the east and west elevations in a nod to the corrugated metal of farm structures.

Perhaps the most palpable distinction between Sixteen Doors and Confluence House is the latter's handling of visibility. Standing just behind a natural berm paralleling a road, the newer 1,650-square-foot building follows a natural east–west axis to overlook a sloping meadow, and its roof extends beyond the building envelope on both long sides to mitigate exposure: facing south, the eave projects well beyond the inhabitable volume to prevent the hottest sun from hitting fenestration; on the largely shielded north elevation, the eave is just deep enough to effect privacy from passing traffic. Minimalist porches wrap beneath each.

The two houses do share ambiguity. Rolston considered how local barns' symmetry and lack of formal entrance made them appear rooted in the local landscape, and Sixteen Doors and Confluence House accordingly eschew formal front doors. Any

of their sliding doors could play the threshold. "Without being self-conscious, it dislodges the house from a nuclear family construct and makes it part of a broader history of building," Rolston says of the design decision.

Another point in common: Rolston subtracted nuclear-family signifiers from the interior scheme. A traditional center hall, walled-off kitchen, and oversize master suite felt out of sync with the Hudson Valley's progressive weekenders and transplants, and with demographic change generally. In Sixteen Doors and Confluence House alike, master and guest bedrooms are interchangeable termini in the floor plan. Between them, an open gathering space encourages casual circulation and transparency of household roles.

"Sixteen Doors is more a building than a piece of architecture; tweak the material palette and shape and it could live comfortably in many environs," Rolston reflects with understatement. "Confluence House, on the other hand, really belongs upstate in the way the porches and roofs manage climate, receive the landscape, and evoke the cow barn." Whether yielding versatile shelter or site-specific architecture, Rolston's archetype makes a strong impression, by embracing agricultural iconography and flouting domestic conventions all at once.

—
An eave and porch, connected into a continuous band, projects from the house's south elevation.

—

"Confluence House belongs upstate in the way the porches and roofs manage climate, receive the landscape, and evoke the cow barn."

—
Looking across the living area (left) and into a bedroom
from the north porch (right).

—
The short sides of Confluence House are finished in
standing-seam metal cladding.

BarlisWedlick Architects namesake Dennis Wedlick has contributed invaluably to architects' quest for a modern Hudson Valley vocabulary. In the mid-1980s, while he was on Philip Johnson's staff, Wedlick began designing affordable housing in Columbia County, New York, as well as a retreat for himself and partner Curt DeVito in Kinderhook. Since Wedlick's moonlighting turned into a full-time entrepreneurship in 1992, his residences have sprung up across the region. Together these projects run the gamut from accurate recreations to postmodernist projects to more rigorous abstractions. They also express an increasingly nuanced understanding of iconography, environmental stewardship, and social equity.

Alan Barlis, who became a co-owner of the studio in 2005, is leading its next moves forward. Meanwhile, Wedlick has applied his status as architectural statesman to inspiring use. From BarlisWedlick's office in Hudson and a newer home in Stanfordville, he designs sustainable housing for the rural workforce through Habitat for Humanity and other not-for-profits. Here Wedlick and Barlis discuss their once and future Hudson Valley.

Conversation with
Alan Barlis & Dennis Wedlick

—
(From left) Dennis
Wedlick and Alan
Barlis.

You describe residences as empathetic to
the people who live in them. Your Hudson
Valley commissions also visibly channel the
forms and intelligence of historic buildings
in the region. How do you square these
two forces?

That's reflected by a certain
lightheartedness in your work.

These clients, many of whom are New
York–based artists, have also allowed
you to delve deeply into sustainability.

One of your personal awakenings to
sustainability took place here, and
it wasn't exactly magical.

How has that lesson translated to
designing homes?

DW   Alan and I liken it to method acting. In Columbia County in particular, we
       want to understand the way our clients see that place. And the history,
       the preserved landscape, the quality of light, and the tremendous wildlife
       and vegetation speak to them. Our work doesn't have a strict vernacular
       feel, because we're not designing for the history of the place, but we are
       designing for people who are influenced by that history.

AB   History is very palpable to our clients, [especially] compared to a place like
       Colorado, where material and labor scarcity is a concern and homeowners
       are happy to be protected from the elements. Issues of domesticity and
       bliss come to the fore in the Hudson Valley. Here the climate is temperate
       enough for people to have inscribed their desires into the landscape.

DW   It's a romantic place, a Rip van Winkle place. In many cases, clients come
       here from New York to clear out their brains from the din of metropolitan
       life. I think that allows us to propose very playful solutions.

DW   That is tied to the magic of the Hudson Valley. The conservation movement
       was born here, and it prevails today without a whit of self-interest.

DW   When Curt and I started out in Kinderhook, we planted daffodils and grass,
       because we were raised to believe that that's how you make places more
       beautiful. It all died. So we thought, What if we were to stop trying to make
       the woods pretty? The lesson is to let the landscape take care of itself.

DW   Do no harm. I want to make sure buildings tread as lightly as possible
       on the earth. We used to want to harness the sun and the wind, and to
       somehow make the boundary between inside and outside disappear in the
       process. But nature, I've learned, wants as little to do with you as possible.
       It wants you to be as self-contained as possible. So if you're going to
       introduce something artificial into the environment, you need to minimize
       its consumption of natural resources.

The BarlisWedlick
Architects–
designed Rural
Compound
project.

Was it that systemic perspective
that led to the Hudson Passive
Project (HPP) in 2010?

A view of Rural
Compound's living
area illustrates
a one-to-one
correspondence
between architec-
tural gesture and
interior volume.

Since HPP, your studio has
become a champion of Passive
House standards.

Dennis, supporting Habitat is now
your full-time responsibility?

AB   We have tried using off-the-shelf materials and thinking small, prefab construction—whatever we could think of to minimize abusing the land. But they weren't necessarily adding up to a whole. I think I've introduced a more systemic approach to that goal.

DW   At the start of the Great Recession, we had just finished an energy-efficient prefabricated home. Then the crash came and we had some time on our hands. The Passive House movement was just coming over from Germany at the time, but there wasn't much data to prove its value, so Alan suggested we do a case study—to make the exact same house according to Passive House efficiency criteria and then perform a side-by-side comparison. With the help of a grant from New York State, we produced HPP, which turned out to consume 99 percent less energy for heating than the prefab version. It also cost $3,000 less to construct.

AB   It was a turning point, because the absence of a client allowed us to study every best practice in our portfolio and make them work in combination to achieve Passive House standards. Since then we've been fortunate to have clients who allow us to apply that knowledge to a lot of different project types, styles, and labor pools. Passive House is now subsumed within best practices.

DW   To that point, Habitat for Humanity asked us if we could achieve something similar to HPP for their families. We had always wanted to share sustainability with that wider audience. Without the volunteerism and other components that Habitat brings to the table, we could never have gotten it to the right price point.

DW   Alan teaches and keeps pushing the envelope in our bread-and-butter business, and I'm this little mouse that just keeps taking from that effort and helping people in our community tap into the knowledge base.

—
The Hudson
Passive Project,
a case study in
energy efficiency
spearheaded by
the architects.

**Has the partnership with
Habitat informed your approach
to sustainability elsewhere?**

**The common person deserves
empathetic design, too.**

—
An interior
view of Hudson
Passive Project.

**Alan, how has your experience in the
Hudson Valley informed the studio's
larger body of work?**

—
BarlisWedlick's
design of the
project considers
ecological
responsibility
and livability.

DW   My whole attitude about sustainability has shifted. In all the work we had been doing before, the form is an integral part of ecological performance. Now, thanks to using volunteer labor and off-the-shelf products, sustainability is all about craftsmanship and materials. That shift has allowed high-performance building to be much more accessible to the common person.

DW   Yes, and that expands the definition of sustainability. Families are moving from homes where they spent $1,000 a month on heating, and now they spend $40 a month for all utility costs. That difference is a trip to the dentist, a computer for your son or daughter, a third job that you may be able to give up to spend time with your family or unplug or be playful. Getting people into housing that's not only affordable to acquire but also unbelievably inexpensive to maintain is empowering for them, and it shows just how connected we feel to the people of this county.

AB   I think there's a basic method at the core of our work. We spend a lot of time with our clients understanding their desires and how they want to live their lives, then helping them dream how architecture and building practices can create the best places for them. That dreaming comes more easily in a place like Columbia County. The farmhouses, well-worn paths, and vistas encourage thinking about one's place in the world—about what is durable physically as well as emotionally.

Natori Residence

Calvin Tsao and Zack McKown's expertise in the Hudson Valley's vernacular architecture is based on firsthand knowledge. Since purchasing a farm in Rhinebeck, New York, in 1998, the founders of Brooklyn-based Tsao & McKown Architects have devoted their spare weekends and vacations to restoring a diminutive 1850s-era gatehouse there. Their longtime clients Josie and Ken Natori also have specialized in the subject, as owners of an eighteenth-century warren of rooms in Pound Ridge. The new residence these collaborators erected on the Natoris' property in 2015 is an antidote to the feelings of confinement that historic homes often kindle.

Tsao & McKown's service to the Natoris spans more than two decades, from homes in New York City and Palm Beach to the offices and showrooms of Josie Natori's eponymous fashion brand. Navigating project types, locations, and time, "We have come to know their habits and their aspirations," Tsao says.

The Pound Ridge commission was hatched as much as a rejoinder to the Natoris' Manhattan residence as to their Pound Ridge antique. In a combination of apartments that Tsao & McKown completed in 2005, only so many structural encumbrances could be removed from the existing building, and husband and wife found themselves sequestered in a study and boudoir to do their daily work. "We got a sense they wanted to spend more time together even as they were doing different things," Tsao

recalls. Two years later, the couple decided to gift the original Pound Ridge house to their grown son and replace it with something more loft-like.

Today the Natori Residence stands on a glacial ledge on the western edge of the 30-acre site, south of the historic house. The single-story rectilinear volume is constructed of strongly figured timber measuring five bays long by two bays wide. Enclosed in expanses of glass, it is oriented for eastern views across an open field to a pond, and shielded by thick pine forest to the west and south. The visibly joined wood system evokes old-growth tree trunks, and it works in tandem with the building's relatively petite dimensions to minimize walls within the 2,900-square-foot space.

—
A traditional Japanese garden surrounds part of the Natori Residence,
serving as a meeting point between built and natural environments.

159

The open interior is modulated into zones, most notably thanks to two large standing-seam copper skylights that rise above the northern end of the flat roof. The asymmetrical, pyramidal forms are glazed only on their north and east faces to prevent too much daylight from penetrating the common areas below. From within, their controlled illumination and sensation of volume demarcate living and dining functions. A custom bronze chimney suspends into the living area, and a granite hearth placed atop a wire-brushed white oak pedestal acknowledges the chimney from below, to further distinguish that space without visually separating occupants from one another. A second fireplace graces the master suite.

Because the Natoris desired closeness to landscape, as well, the architects ran a timber-columned veranda along the living and dining areas on the east elevation to encourage indoor-outdoor use. Meanwhile, a terrace off the master suite blends into the landscape in interlocking planes of natural materials, and a traditional Japanese garden wraps around the west elevation, drawing a person outside and inviting her to explore the various vignettes. Tsao notes that these elements "start conversations about the built environment and the natural environment."

Neither client's nor architect's historic homes would understand this dialogue on enclosure and mediation, wilderness and artifice. Reflecting on his and McKown's Rhinebeck gatehouse, Tsao explains the brick structure sprouted a clapboard addition at the turn of the twentieth century to contain a kitchen: "In every vernacular, there is an objective first. The gatehouse has masonry mass, so it's cool in the summer, and the kitchen generated enough heat that it could effectively be an outhouse building of light wood construction with many windows. Buildings had to consider a relationship with the outdoors to keep the elements out. From those strategies, an aesthetic emerges."

In a generation when a building's technology can effectively protect a home from weather conditions and wear and tear, according to this reasoning an architect would replicate aesthetic merely to honor heritage. The Natori Residence, then, respects the Hudson Valley's historic architecture in method rather than form. As Tsao puts it, "It represents a no-nonsense way of thinking about your needs and resolving them."

—
The garden's water element is the threshold to a formal entry.

—
A narrow floorplate minimizes structural elements in the
interior, and maximizes its interaction with the outdoors.

—

The Natori Residence respects the Hudson Valley's historic architecture in method rather than form.

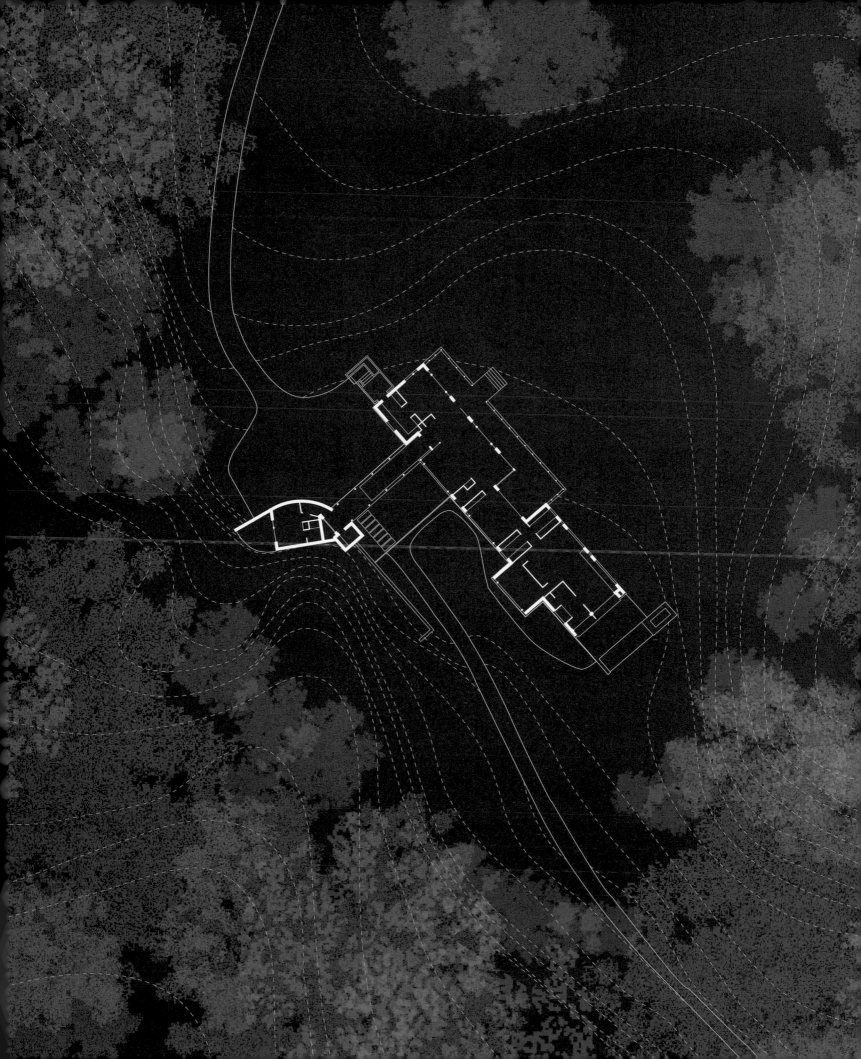

—
The architecture subtly demarcates different vignettes
within the living area.

—
Two views showing how open planning and porosity with
landscape carry into the master suite.

—

Skylights above the common interiors impart a memorable
roofscape to the project, and shape the experience within.

Old
Field
Farm

From his arrival in New York City in 1976, Peter Nadin forged his career with creative integrity. The British-born artist achieved success in collaborations that bypassed style and collector trends, and his solo endeavors followed the heart rather than the market. But perhaps Nadin refused categorization within the art scene most emphatically by stepping away from it: Upon concluding an exhibition of paintings at Yale's Center for British Art in 1992, he decided to stop showing work and, as *New York Times* writer Randy Kennedy chronicled in an expansive profile, "he became, for all intents and purposes, a farmer, sitting out an era in which the art world . . . [became] increasingly driven by the demands of commerce and popular culture."

Nadin arranged his hiatus at Old Field Farm, which he and his wife, Art + Commerce cofounder Anne Kennedy, had purchased shortly after the bicentennial of the property in 1984. Located near the Catskills in Cornwallville, New York, the partly reforested site allowed the couple to adjust to agricultural life meditatively. In the turn-of-the-last-century farmhouse, Kennedy and Nadin took on new duties—beekeeping followed by gardening, then animal husbandry—with an ethic and deliberateness that today are exemplary of the locavore and sustainable farming movements.

Old Field Farm represented a kind of artistic residency for Nadin to reconsider the point and pace of his work, but he decamped from New York only psychically. He continued teaching at Cooper Union while Kennedy attended to her Manhattan-based photography agency, and in 1996 the couple purchased a townhouse in Greenwich Village as an urban base.

Kennedy and Nadin approached architect Michael Haverland two years later, when they decided to do something about the grandfathered toolshed standing neglected behind the townhouse. Feeling a kinship with the way Haverland had adapted historical modernism to residences in the Hamptons, they commissioned him to create a 220-square-foot pavilion in the toolshed's place. The process yielded a steel-and-glass jewel box, and an invitation to Old Field Farm.

It was 2005 and, Haverland recalls, Nadin was preparing to increase agricultural production, to make art solely from harvested materials. He and Kennedy had just purchased an adjacent property uphill and to the west of the farmhouse, to reconstitute Old Field Farm's original 160 acres, and they asked the architect to develop a master plan for the entire plot. Haverland was to plan and conceive an artist's studio, large greenhouse, and farm manager's office and apartment, as well as outbuildings and outdoor spaces.

The greenhouse, studio, and newest archive building (left to right) designed by Michael Haverland for artist Peter Nadin.

A barn-like studio and kit greenhouse were the initial puzzle pieces to come to life. Ascribing a vernacular character to the pair of buildings "was nearly an automatic choice," Haverland explains. "The amount of snow obliged a pitched-roof structure, and installing a foreign presence would not have been responsible to the historic landscape." In plan the two buildings form a slight hinge around the pond where Nadin grows kemp and bamboo for art paper.

How should the casual observer reconcile Old Field Farm with Haverland's Greenwich Village or Hamptons commissions, which appear to have more in common with Adolf Loos and Le Corbusier than Old MacDonald? The architect responds that all his projects reflect the teachings of his mentors, famed postmodernists Robert Venturi and Denise Scott Brown, irrespective of one house's style versus another's. Postmodernism champions the architectural image of a place, Haverland explains, "and Venturi specifically talks about the complexity and contradiction of that image—between what it seems and what it really is." As for how appearance and reality differ in the case of Old Field Farm, Nadin's studio, for example, "just looks like another barn from a distance, but as you get closer the details are unexpected."

Scrutiny of Old Field Farm produces several revelations to that end. Nadin's 2,000-square-foot studio features facing mahogany doors that soar to fourteen feet high, a dimension that somersaults

traditional barn buildings and which blurs inside and out. And ancillary structures that rarely demand unexpected detailing, let alone much thought, sport innovations: chicken coops are outfitted with tractor wheels, so that droppings may fertilize swaths of pasture on rotation; the greenhouse is geothermally heated.

The architect recognizes Kennedy and Nadin as mentors on this project, as well, citing, "I no longer presume that an obvious material solution is the best solution. You can use labor-intensive methods that are still cost-effective." Materials and labor were selected with intense purposefulness because the clients wanted to build in a regional, precorporate manner consistent with their farming. The studio's scissor-truss structure is a product of hemlock trees felled on site, and Amish carpenters made the tall mahogany doors a few miles away.

The intellectual influence has been mutual. After almost two decades away from the scene, in 2011 Nadin showed his locavore art as the series *First Mark* at Gavin Brown's Enterprise to positive reviews. "For Nadin, art finds form in agriculture," critic Linda Yablonsky wrote, adding that the exhibition "symbolizes Nadin's return to the fold and represents the path that led him out of it." Further recognizing the essential role that Old Field Farm has played in the creative journey, Nadin, Kennedy, and Haverland more recently realized an amendment to the master plan—a building where Nadin is archiving his work.

The buildings are configured in part to frame distant views
of the property and landscape.

—

Old Field Farm represented a kind of artistic residency for Nadin to reconsider the point and pace of his work.

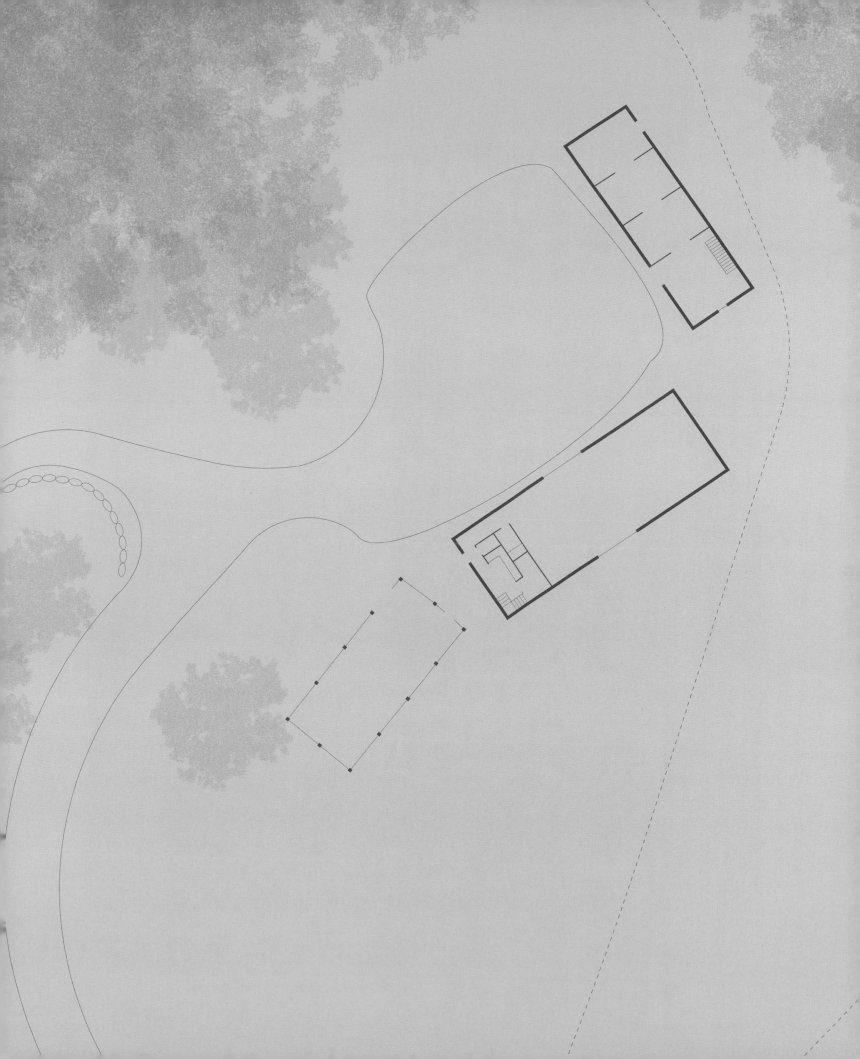

Corresponding exterior and interior views of the
archive building.

Looking out from the studio.

Haverland operates one of the fourteen-foot doors
gracing Nadin's studio.

Dutchess County Art Barn

Barns are the muse of Hudson Valley design: relics are transformed into residences, or the building type informs ground-up efforts. Dutchess County Art Barn touches down between these poles of reuse and quotation. For the Millerton, New York, project, Manhattan-based architect Matthew Baird reinvented an all-new agricultural product as a 6,000-square-foot home.

Baird's client originally envisioned modernizing a barn as part of a larger residence. But history rarely deposited barns on the remote hillside that the couple had desired. And Baird nixed the prospect of transporting one to an idyllic spot as disingenuous. Deciding that fantastic site trumped restoration, in 2007 the client purchased a 110-acre former dairy farm overlooking Mount Stissing and the Catskills. Meanwhile, the architect began work on an entirely new compound comprising a pair of houses and a storage structure.

The subprime crisis that soon followed forced a reckoning of priorities yet again. "The project no longer felt conscionable as friends were losing their jobs," Baird recalls. Architect and client contemplated tabling the project altogether, or abbreviating it to suit chastened times.

During this critical juncture, Baird made a routine trip to a nearby Agway store, which unexpectedly informed a path forward. "There I saw an advertisement for pre-engineered steel run-in sheds, and a light bulb went off that we could capture a lot of square footage for not much money." The design process restarted with Baird adapting one of these horse stalls into the client's storage facility. As the husband and wife's enthusiasm for the scheme mounted, Baird doubled its square footage to contain almost all the functions of the original compound.

—
A slot within Dutchess County Art Barn's north elevation
includes the formal entrance.

189

Baird consulted with manufacturer Star Building Systems as it executed the final building design in 2011, which the architect laughingly calls "a 125-by-25-by-30-foot shoebox." Today a visitor ascends a patchwork of reforested land and extant meadows to be greeted by a wall of Cor-Ten on the house's short north elevation, which is slotted near one corner to include a formal entrance. The weathering steel also runs the length of the east, summit-facing elevation, where industrial-scale garage doors conjure the equestrian.

A combination of glass and polycarbonate clads the west and south elevations. These two sides meet at a mahogany-framed curtain wall that floods the double-height living room immediately behind it in daylight and views. Several glass panels in this corner slide open, as well, to place occupants more directly within a garden-ringed lawn designed by Wagner Hodgson Landscape Architecture.

Baird pulled the Art Barn interior's second floor away from the polycarbonate skin to produce the soaring living room, and he drew that gap along the west elevation toward the front door to create an entry gallery. Exterior materials correspond to the functions within, as common spaces hem to the visually lightweight facades and private interiors are sheathed more opaquely. "Those decisions were driven equally by place," Baird adds, pointing out how Cor-Ten and polycarbonate reflect "the expression of the woods and the views, the industrial versus the organic, and the blurring of inside and out."

If regionalist contemporary design honors traditional local construction, then Dutchess County Art Barn refutes a notion that only the handcrafted architecture of yesteryear is to be celebrated. As Baird puts it, "People are often searching for an ideal barn form, and there is a beauty to knowing that a completely efficient and purposeful structure is already in production and accessible at a local farm supplier." The Millerton residence embodies that claim to uplifting effect.

—

The building's Cor-Ten and polycarbonate facades meet in its northwest corner.

—

Exterior materials correspond to the functions within, as common spaces hem to the visually lightweight facades and private interiors are sheathed more opaquely.

Looking west and south from the living room (left).
The western panorama (right).

The residence overlooks a western lawn, while the overall
property measures 110 acres.

House
432

The southeastern edge of the Hudson Valley defies clear definition. In this meeting of New York and Connecticut, the terrain varies between ridges and bowls, and is covered alternately in woods and meadows. One town's primary intersection resembles a New England square while another's is marked only by the crisscrossing of stone walls. Revolutionary-era shingled and clapboard houses huddle along the roads; bedroom communities loom over them from once-unbuildable prospects.

Katonah, New York–based architect Robert Siegel revels in these regional juxtapositions. The house he designed for himself, his wife Lynn, and their three children assimilates local knottiness into a deceptively simple diagram. "My intent was to design a house that appeared anchored and inevitable, almost as if it had always been here," Siegel says.

House 432's site embodies all the complexity of the border zone, as the plot once served as the brick lot of the estate of John Jay, first chief justice of the United States Supreme Court. Jay had established the property as an income-producing farm in 1787, and at its peak it measured well over a square mile of fields and formal grounds. Parcels were sold off as New York City crept northward: At about the same time the homestead opened to the public in 1964, four acres were carved from its southeastern corner to sprout a suburban house in a roughly colonial style.

The Siegels purchased that residence in 2011, smitten less by it and more the undulating topography on which it sat. They coveted south-facing open space located behind and above the house as a new construction site. Yet because the existing building was perfectly serviceable, the family decided to tear it down in as responsible a fashion as possible. It donated all the house's contents to local nonprofits, and then allowed the Katonah Fire Department to train on the structure. Firefighters conducted one final controlled burn on the midcentury house in March 2014, shortly after construction of its 3,600-square-foot replacement had been substantially completed at a safe remove.

—
House 432's extensive stonework pays homage to
centuries-old local building techniques.

Besides cresting the Siegels' desired spot, the hilltop building maximizes distance from the road, which runs along the southern border of the property. That move has the very practical benefit of mitigating traffic noise, and affirms a larger Western design tradition. "The building is only one part of the landscape," the architect explains of that legacy. "It makes space with the site, attracts movement through the landscape, and engages the landscape from within it."

Site plan, building plan, and section all privilege the landscape, in turn. Siegel traced the entry sequence with simple stone walls that transition to a low courtyard partly enclosed by a service building and the main house's south elevation, drawing the eye from south to north. To modulate the scale of the four-bedroom residence, Siegel angled and tapered its L-shaped footprint into a slight boomerang shape to keep it from visually dominating the hill. The approach to fenestration—of punching few, though very large, apertures into the envelope—further dials back the house's appearance. Perhaps the most overt nod to landscape is the locally sourced stone that clads the house exterior from top to bottom, though this naturalistic cloak also has fun with the area's historic stone walls by turning structure into skin.

Disconnecting from the visual blights and excess noise of the manmade world informs one's direct, haptic experience of the design, too. The crunching of driveway gravel beneath car tires, or the tinkling of water in the patio tucked between the garage and main house, refocuses multiple senses to the world of home. Upon arrival, the spare windows select only the most bracing views of landscape to frame from within. Interior elements that could have been standard-issue are instead gestures to family life: a floating stair skirts the living room to host kids' impromptu performances; the kitchen fully integrates eating and dining; a second-floor setback and parapet are refashioned into a private courtyard for stargazing. The effect is seclusion without parochialism.

Looking back on House 432's design, Siegel says he grappled with a riddle of contemporary architectural practice of which inevitability is one part, and artistic expression is the other. "How do you design a home that looks unique, but not out of place—how do you understand context without being a slave to it?" This project's answer is to filter local and historical cues through the lens of personal haven. As Katonah and the lower Hudson Valley become more aggressively suburban, Siegel's method for inserting a new dream home in the landscape is hearteningly thoughtful.

—
Architect Robert Siegel employed a variety of secondary
structures to guide occupants toward the entry.

—

"How do you design a home that looks unique, but not out of place?"

—
Sweeping living and dining spaces (left) include a stair whose broad landings and screen-like
vertical element can serve as a family stage (right).

Hidden enclaves like a rooftop courtyard encourage
family interaction.

—
House 432 sits atop the highest point on the 4-acre parcel.

Ex of In House

Widely regarded as a trailblazer of modern architecture, Steven Holl has come a long way from the small projects and unbuilt concepts that first captured the attention of the design world. Nowadays, in the rare lull between client meetings and topping-out ceremonies, Holl will still engage in the speculation that helped make his name. Ex of In House, located near the New York–based architect's longtime weekend home in Rhinebeck, represents one of those recent pursuits. Completed in 2016, the building is an experiment in space making—and a touch of social engineering—conducted at domestic scale.

At its outset, Holl had not intended to erect a house. Over the course of architectural history, a fascination with intersecting spheres has united thinkers as chronologically disparate as Étienne-Louis Boullée and Antti Lovag, and Holl decided to expand upon this centuries-long dialogue in a spare moment. While working alongside his R&D team to imagine various three-dimensional Venn Diagrams, he received word that a Rhinebeck neighbor, on the verge of retirement, was advertising his 28-acre property as a five-plot subdivision.

The whiff of development rankled him. "I believe in preserving as much of the natural landscape as possible," Holl says. He also notes that that ethic dates to his early, research-centric career. "Years ago, my big manifesto had to do with the edge of the city. I devised this whole project about clarifying the rural landscape and having it meet densely packed city structures." He bought the Rhinebeck acreage in 2014 to preclude suburbanization. He also determined that his investigation of spheres was so rich with potential that an iteration of it should be installed there.

Before he could proceed with Ex of In House, Holl had to iron out a technicality of local zoning. His scheme had to conform to principal dwelling, meaning that a preexisting structure on the site had to be renovated as an accessory structure. That 1959 cabin functioned as a traditional hunting blind, from which occupants aim at their quarry in concealment. Holl reconceived its fenestration as so-called light turrets—a series of large portals and daylight collectors—transforming the overall dynamic of man preying upon nature into a reverence for ecology. If Holl could not limit the site to one building footprint, he could at least minimize the sense of human dominion.

—
Architect Steven Holl initiated Ex of In House to prevent the
underlying acreage from becoming subdivided.

215

That ambition informed the sculpting of the all-new dwelling, too. Employing a partial tesseract in addition to spheres, Holl arranged Ex of In House's slanted volumes and circular and wedge-shaped windows to again ingratiate built environment with the sun. Glazing on the south elevation is proportioned to heat the interior by thermal gain in winter, for example, and glass flooring meets a dramatic window on the southwest corner so that sunsets are experienced without interruption. A geothermal system, super-insulated envelope, thin-film photovoltaics, and other active sustainability efforts reduce the house to almost net-zero consumption, consistent with Holl's desire to tread lightly on the planet.

The boundary-pushing interior arguably evidences this ethic most. Holl's shifting planes and kissing orbs create an interior landscape that contains only one door, and feels much larger than 918 square feet. "There is something special about this house, which is very hard to explain," Holl says. One pragmatic explanation is that, within the nooks and crannies of the complex geometry, Holl can insert a kitchen or imply partitions in a way that any other house sleeping five cannot. Compactness is an inherently ecological gesture, and this version of it uses volumetric potential to optimize area.

Ex of In House is, ultimately, a statement of optimism overall. Its very existence embodies Holl's belief that the moral universe will arc toward land conservation, resource efficiency, and art. The wide-open layout also expresses faith that guests can tolerate or even thrive in an interior world that lacks borders. But there is something inexplicably polemical about this research project come to life, as well. It suggests that other houses, even the sensitively modernist ones, have gobbled up too much of the Hudson Valley. Perhaps Ex of In House and the powerhouse architect behind it will start righting that imbalance in nature's favor.

—

The house's southwest corner features a giant porthole window that wraps
two elevations and extends below the second floor.

—

If Holl could not limit the site to one building footprint, he could at least minimize the sense of human dominion.

—
Viewing the entrance from the second-floor porthole (above)
and from its adjacent sitting area (opposite).

—
Sleeping areas are hidden out of direct sight of the
second floor.

223

—
Ex of In House measures a mere 918 square feet.

Since spending childhood summers in Maine, the New Orleans–born, New York–based architect Drew Lang has known the pleasures of rural respite. Having even a toehold in nature alleviates the pressures of city life, he says. Since Lang launched his eponymous firm in 2003, he also has become fluent in real estate development. In order to better compensate its employees and ride out billing cycles, Lang Architecture generates projects that it designs, constructs, and sells on its own.

Personal and professional narratives intersected in 2011, when Lang first scouted 131 acres of mature forest in Kerhonkson, New York. On this spot adjacent to the Shawangunk Mountains and overlooking the Roundout Valley, Lang and investors laid the groundwork for Hudson Woods, a twenty-six-parcel development in which homeowners would purchase a version of Lang's 2,300-square-foot model house with their lot. Just as *subdivision* does not convey the daintiness with which this project team intervened in the landscape, so *spec house* is wrongly suggestive. Lang's gable-roofed design pays regard to vernacular buildings; extensive use of bluestone extracted from a historic quarry on site embraces place directly.

Within two years of the model house's 2014 completion, all but four of its kin had become reality, with a majority of them occupied by New York–area creative professionals. Here, Lang reflects on Hudson Woods and its positive reception.

Conversation with
Drew Lang

Architect
Drew Lang

What prompted you to go into the business of second homes?

So first came the development idea, and then you determined that the Hudson Valley would be the place for it?

You can sense this energy in the many historic house rehabilitations that have taken place.

And what would a Hudson Woods house cost as a one-off?

Did anything make this project more difficult than expected?

Would you describe the process at which you arrived at a model house?

DL I simply observed that a lot of people wanted an escape to nature, but didn't know how to achieve it, because it seemed prohibitive in terms of cost, time, or process.

DL I drew a 100-mile-radius circle around New York but kept coming back to this part of the Hudson Valley, because it's stunningly beautiful and there's a wealth of unspoiled land available, as well as preserved land. I also sensed a budding energy in the area. I was warned that that energy had been around since the peak of the Catskills resorts and the advent of affordable air travel. Yet I believed in it.

DL Yes, but as charming as they are, old houses require significant maintenance that many homeowners don't want to be inconvenienced by. The common alternative of architects doing new, one-off projects for individual clients is inefficient, too. We said we'd only go forward with this alternative if we could deliver an excellent new product for a low price.

DL It would cost double, which we know empirically based on our work with individual clients.

DL The site work was number one. I wasn't willing to sacrifice nature. So bit by bit, we surgically carved away just enough to place infrastructure and homes within nature. That's very complex, though the objective is to look like it was always meant to be. Being naïve was a blessing in this sense. There's a reason why developers buy a flat piece of land, clear it tabula rasa, and build up from there.

DL The evolution of a design is never linear. I always had a connection to extant buildings, place, and landscape, and here we put down this form that definitely borrows from agricultural architecture. Then you question yourself, How do we bridge past and present? How do we make a modern home instead of a barn or shed?

Hudson Woods
comprises 26 lots
on 131 acres.

**How much did repetition inform
the design?**

**Were you concerned about
repetition leading to homogeneity?**

Each Hudson
Woods home is
based on a model
of Lang's design.

**If there had been no constraints—no desire
to beat the price of a one-off residence,
no logic in systematizing the design, or no
demand to return on investment—would
Hudson Woods look and feel different?**

**What else has trumped
your anticipation?**

The Hudson Woods
prototype reconciled
cabin aesthetics
with the legacy of
modernism.

DL   We had to come up with a design that was systematic, easy to understand, and straightforward to build twenty-six times. A lot of ideas would make their way into the drawings and get thrown out, as a result. Though that's generally the way any design process works.

DL   It was a question among our first buyers, and we were honestly concerned about it, too. But we trusted in the diverse and dramatic landscape. The elevation differential across the property is more than 200 feet, and the houses appear more distinct than even I anticipated. There is a cohesion to everything, too—you could argue that the essential repetition is a kind of integration with the landscape.

DL   Unquestionably different, but not dramatically so. I do wonder if absolute freedom would have brought us to do a flat-roofed house, because there's no question that a flat roof has a more modern reading, albeit less broad appeal, than a gable shape. We would have had to change the volume altogether in that case. Now, the flat roof nicely suits a small structure like the pool house, which appears in conversation with the main volume.

DL   There's an inherent sense of community at Hudson Woods. Homeowners share this deep interest in the place, and from that commonality they want to connect with one another. This project has also drawn a lot of people to the studio—anti-developers like us who have incredible properties and refined sensibilities, and who see a relationship between their vision and what we've done in the foothills of the Catskills.

Hudson
Guest House

Asked whether the Hudson Valley has an architectural language all its own, architect Hal Goldstein responds, "The identity is forming, though isn't it crazy that it hasn't formed already? I don't know why the whole Hudson Valley isn't Napa."

Mount Merino may very well be the place where this identity incubates. In 1860 the artist Frederic Edwin Church—who led the second generation of the Hudson River School after Thomas Cole's death in 1848—bought a 126-acre farm near the summit of Mount Merino, and tapped both Richard Morris Hunt and Calvert Vaux to help him design structures for the property. The site would ultimately double in size and mature into the long-beloved estate Olana, and it has since spawned flights of architectural fancy nearby. In 2015, Goldstein's Manhattan-based firm Janson Goldstein contributed to this milieu, with the completion of a guest house near Mount Merino's lower peak.

The 1,000-square-foot building accompanies an existing gray stucco house that Goldstein describes as "wonderfully situated on the top of the hill overlooking the valley" and whose bold roofline and stucco walls convey a strong presence. The new homeowners required more space to accommodate guests as well as a gym, and the design team chose to add that functionality without duplication; "our approach was to create an object that stood in its own right, as a complement to the main house," Goldstein explains.

The new rectilinear volume was installed northeast of the original residence, and clad in cedar with copper edging. The cedar was painted a charcoal that approximates the color of a shadow in the landscape. Meanwhile, facing planes of floor-to-ceiling glass on the long elevations lighten the appearance of the small building and make its central common room appear almost like a breezeway. In a similar vein, Janson Goldstein notched out the southwest corner of the volume while leaving the structural assembly visible, resulting in a minimalist colonnade. The gym is tucked into the short blunt panhandle of the remaining unglazed space, and a bedroom is located at the opposite end.

—
Hudson Guest House is sited on four acres atop a
peak of Mount Merino.

Besides turning residential tropes into delicate abstractions, Janson Goldstein's design melds indoors and out. The colonnade, which opens into the common room, mediates between the hilltop meadow and architectural imprint. Sandwiched between walls of glass, the living area flows into the grassy landscape rather than seeks refuge from it. Distant mountains are visible to the northwest, but one must crane a neck to see the main house. "We did not want to compete with it or blur its clarity," Goldstein says of the primary building.

The project ultimately adds more clarity to the residence. "The guesthouse serves as a beacon for drivers wending up this part of Mount Merino, and as you turn into the property, it effectively says hello to you, as well," Goldstein says. The main house and its subtle counterpart also ring two sides of an entry court, so that wayfinding becomes more intuitive for the newcomer. Viewed alongside an east-facing 20-by-45-foot pool and deck that Janson Goldstein completed simultaneously, the guesthouse maximizes the experience of the hilltop—encouraging exploration of the 4-acre site and various architectural expressions embedded within it. It transforms the residence into an unpretentious, writ-small Olana of our time.

—
A delicate, abstract colonnade identifies the building's
formal entry.

—

"The guest house serves as a beacon for drivers wending up this part of Mount Merino, and as you turn into the property, it effectively says hello to you."

—
Views of the meadow landscape from within and through
the living area.

—
The project's south elevation is divided into opaque, semi-private, transparent, and outdoor zones.

The River House

The concept of "keeping up with the Joneses" may have been born in the Hudson Valley when, in 1853, Elizabeth Schermerhorn Jones's estate Wyndclyffe rewrote the rules of country residences. The imposing Gothic pile on eighty acres of Rhinebeck promontory prompted a spate of mansion building and rebuilding along the Hudson River. Though Wyndclyffe is but a ruin today, it remains a window into an American mindset not entirely bygone.

Wyndclyffe's underlying land was subdivided after its abandonment in 1950, and the home created by Steve Mensch for himself and Greg Patnaude now occupies the former great lawn. The new residence is known as The River House, and it embodies present-day values much as the original Wyndclyffe captured its own time. New is horizontal to the old's vertical; a bracing experience of the riverfront contrasts a romantic object in the landscape; Mensch's design substitutes status with authenticity.

While an observer cannot help reflecting on both Wyndclyffe and The River House as a pair of social benchmarks, Mensch says proximity to the relic did not oblige him to make a commentary. He fashioned the 5,000-square-foot house as a counterpoint to his first Rhinebeck home, a compound whose lush valley acreage focused on a storybook waterfall. "For twenty-two years we loved our private, introverted world," Mensch says of his previous address. Yet family demographics no longer required multiple structures, and the architect yearned for another project: "We wanted to try something extroverted, and something easier to maintain—a Villa Savoye from which we could overlook the Hudson Valley's natural landscape."

There is nothing retiring about the former lawn. The site may as well stand *en pointe*, with enormous southern views of the Hudson that sweep westward and taper to the north. Mensch and Patnaude also wanted to integrate their home with ecological systems, and this outgoing site harvests abundant sunshine. "I take my cues from the site, and in this case, it was very clear I wanted the main spaces to hang over the water as much as possible," the architect says of the ensuing design process. "The rapid slope of the land to the river also allowed me to put the private spaces on a level below the public spaces, which gave me freedom in designing the roof."

—
The first-time visitor to The River House may think the house
simply comprises a rectilinear volume sprouting solar arrays.

Mensch envisioned the approach to the house as a slow, even mysterious procession. The curved driveway is enclosed by high hedges and mature trees, creating a passage to a circular motor court encircled by woods, newly planted spruces, and the board-formed concrete walls of the house itself. These massive, windowless walls could very well be ruins were it not for the delicate, structurally independent steel members holding photovoltaics overhead and signaling a thoughtful pairing of earthen and ethereal.

A covered walkway conveys guests along the concrete to a lone portal. This front door leads to a small, low-ceilinged foyer, where a jog to the left then leads to the fully glazed living room. Over the course of just a few steps, the hint of a bird's-eye Hudson River view transforms into flight itself. "Invariably, when newcomers come through that opening, they gasp, or exclaim, or sometimes just laugh," Mensch says of his impeding, compressing, and finally releasing visitors into the view. The living room's glass walls can retract fully into pockets, to heighten the sense of soaring among treetops.

Because a deck would have compromised the immediacy of the living room's southern vista, the north wall of the room opens onto a flagstone courtyard to provide occupants with an indoor-outdoor connection. Meanwhile, the project's river-facing sides are ringed by a steel catwalk placed thirty inches below the datum, so that constructed edges disappear into the horizon much like an infinity pool. The long concrete entrance wall encloses the east and north sides of the courtyard. It terminates in Mensch's two-story studio, a miniature tower that also sports a steel frame; this crown is inlaid with solar thermal panels.

The living room's sustainable roof produces twenty-eight kilowatts of electricity, more than Mensch and Patnaude need, while the studio's rooftop array produces hot water for the house, heats the pool, and supports radiant interior floors come wintertime; geothermal heat pumps are primarily responsible for heating and cooling. Both rooftop arrays also shade the buildings, lowering air-conditioning loads and protecting glass from summer sun. Mensch notes that they become part of the fundamental imagery of the project, too. Working in tandem with the thoughtful composition at their base, the solar roofs declare The River House's independence from fossil fuels, excessive maintenance, and ceremony—the very things, in other words, that burdened the original Wyndclyffe.

—
The entry elevation exudes gravity and discretion.

—
The building's aerie quality becomes palpable upon entering
the living room, whose glass walls are retractable.

—

"We wanted to try something extroverted, and something easier to maintain—a Villa Savoye from which we could overlook the Hudson Valley's natural landscape."

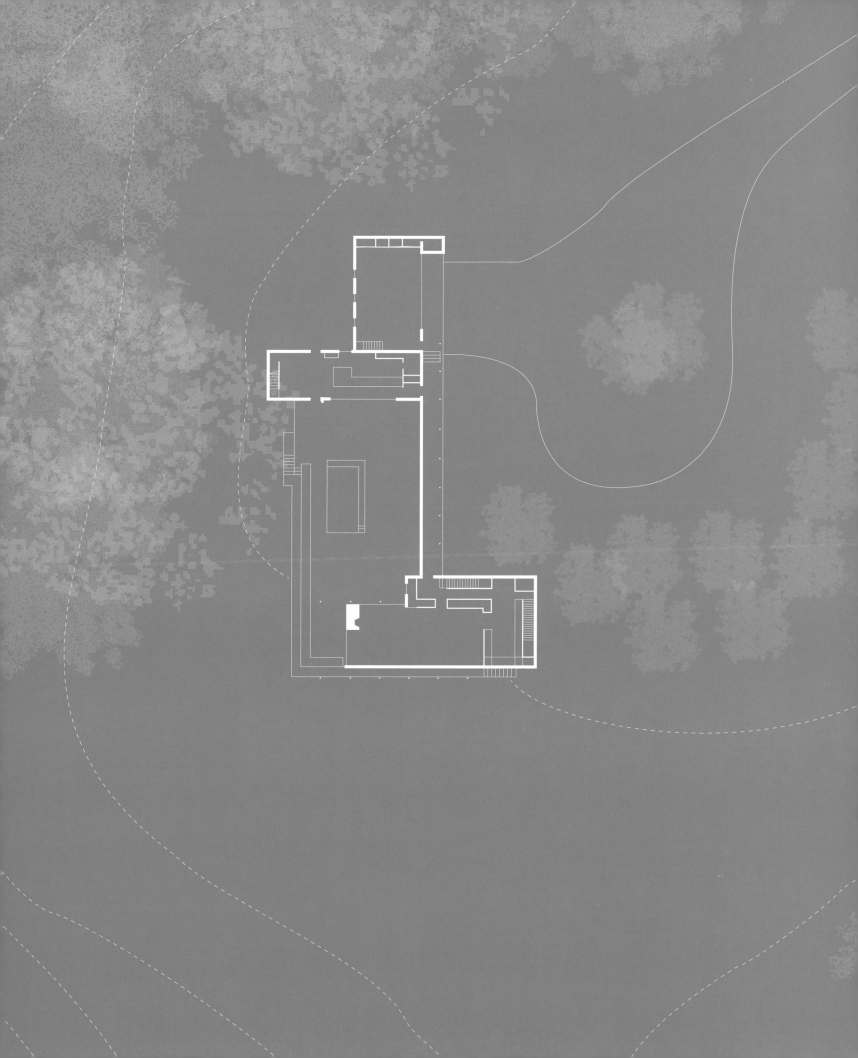

—
A lower level of bedrooms engages the hillside (above), while the two-story
studio building is a treetop space for concentration (opposite).

—
Whereas the living room perches above the dramatic hillside site to the south (above), its north wall opens to a flagstone courtyard where an occupant can experience the outdoors in a more tactile manner (opposite).

—
The photovoltaic array adds formal interest and shade to the inhabitable
volume beneath it; the lower-level bedrooms appear as a plinth.

Acknowledgments

Books are the product of many authors. Were it not for the architects and photographers whose work fills them, these pages could not have existed. I am deeply grateful for the talent and cooperation of not only these men and women, but also of the men and women who support them: Jane Berrill; Christine Cordazzo; John Deitering; Jeannine Diakite; Heidi Engstrom; Jessa Farkas; Emma Hamilton; Caroline Hirsch; Shawn Horn; Michael Kolodesh; Liz Kubany; Stephanie Lim; Jamie McCormick; Larisa Marossine; Jessica Olshen; Dawn Marie Polak; Vicky Saperstein; Catherine Shih; Suzanne Tóth-Pál; Julia van den Hout; Ian Veidenheimer; Carin Whitney; Erika Yorio. Of course, standing behind this entire list are the homeowners. While their names may not be unanimously disclosed, they are role models for anyone who dreams of someday hiring an architect.

Thanks to Annelies De Rouck, Ed Devereux, the Menzies, Stephen Monkarsh, Brent Refsland, Helen Seslowsky, and the others who believed that *Hudson Modern* could find a spot in their respective stores. Thanks also goes to fellow design journalists like Anna Fixsen, Sarah Harrelson, Sheila Kim, Jeremy Lehrer, Linda Lentz, Catherine Osborne, and Dan Rubinstein, whom I am proud to call collaborators and friends, as well as to David Insinga, Renee Pilone, Taylor Lednum, and my other gifted colleagues at GSA. Making a book is a vulnerable act, and your encouragement helped me believe that my ideas about the Hudson Valley were worth sharing, that my words deserved to be printed in big, attention-getting type.

Then there are the people who have wrestled directly with those ideas and words. If *Hudson Modern* finds any success, then it belongs to my editor Alan Rapp and graphic designers Chris Grimley and Anna Driscoll equally. For my family, Ruth Altchek, Leigh Batnick, the Durham boys, Russell Fortmeyer, John Haffner Layden, Tami Hausman, Amy King, John Kriskiewicz, Jacob Rothschild, Adam Thorburn, and Michael Vann, meanwhile, the only incentive to dissect paragraphs or scrutinize Amazon thumbnails was personal fulfillment. Finally, to Rick East, I dedicate this project. I hope its realization brings you profound gratification, in turn.

Credits

© Peter Aaron/OTTO: 41, 42, 46–51, 152, 154, 235, 236, 240–243

Iwan Baan: 67, 68, 72–75, 216, 221

Ty Cole: 228

Deborah DeGraffenreid Photography: 230

B. Docktor: 150

© Pieter Estersohn: 254, 255, 258–259

© Elizabeth Felicella/Esto: 14, 18–21, 194–195

© Brian Ferry: 55, 56, 60–63

Steve Freihon: 113, 114, 118–121

John Halpern: 247, 248, 250, 256–257

Christian Hansen: 90

Laurie Lambrecht: 175, 176, 180–185

Naho Kubota: 79, 80, 84–87, 92, 94

Joshua McHugh: 139, 140, 144–147

Jane Messinger: 125, 126, 130–135

Andrew Rugge: 99, 100, 104–109

Simon Upton: 159, 160, 162–163, 166–171

Paul Warchol: 25, 26, 28–29, 32–37, 201, 202, 206–211, 215, 220, 222–225

Jim Westphalen: 189, 190, 195, 196–197

Mark Wickens: 13

Library of Congress Control Number: 2018933145

ISBN 978-1-58093-484-8

10 9 8 7 6 5 4 3 2 1

Printed in China

Design by Chris Grimley and Anna Driscoll
over,under
www.overunder.co

The Monacelli Press
6 West 18th Street
New York, New York 10011
www.monacellipress.com